THE ROAD TO SUCCESS:

THE ROAD TO SUCCESS:

GAINING HAPPINESS IN A NEW COUNTRY

EDWARD LE

authorHOUSE®

AuthorHouse™
1663 Liberty Drive
Bloomington, IN 47403
www.authorhouse.com
Phone: 1 (800) 839-8640

Published by AuthorHouse 04/15/2015

ISBN: 978-1-5049-0146-8 (sc)
ISBN: 978-1-5049-0147-5 (hc)
ISBN: 978-1-5049-0145-1 (e)

Print information available on the last page.

Dedication

This book is dedicated to my lovely daughter, Katelynh Hoang-Khuyen Le, my parents, all my brothers, sister, friends, and people who love and support me.

I am inspired by the numerous young students who come to the United States to study and start a new life.

Contents

Introduction

In life there are many paths that we can choose, but we should only choose a path that will lead to peace of mind and inner peace.

Sometimes in life two opportunities are presented where both are quantified as true equals. Thing such as deciding where to go to college, which major to study, which job to take. When there are two options presented, it is often difficult to make a decision. We talk to people, we analyze, we think of all the pros and cons of these options. We lose sleep. We talk to friends and family members and listen to their opinions and even wonder why we asked in the first place. But they may not have the right answer or the answer we are looking for. The truth is the answer is deep within our hearts. We just need to listen to it; listen to our heart and find these answers. But we need to go through these experiences and listen to it and also train ourselves so we are ready for it when it comes. We need to prepare for it when the opportunity comes.

Chances are if both options are equally fantastic, then either one will be the right choice. Both will present challenges that are weighted similarly, and both will lead to equally good things. No matter which path you choose, it will lead to other paths, more choices, and a beautiful view along the way.

***

Through my life, I also learned that great opportunities come around every five years. Once the opportunity is gone, then a new opportunity will come. Once we are ready for it, we will have it. Life is an adventure. We will be challenged with opportunities, exploration, and joy if we are ready for it. There will always be opportunities along the way, but we need to be ready for them.

This book will teach you about Vietnamese culture and Asian in general and the adaptation to the U.S.A. culture and the suffering caused by living in a new culture, new country and how to handle it, how to balance the new culture, adapt to it, and find a right path, a direction to reach our final destination, gain happiness and success in life. This book also introduces some of new concepts, ideas and approach to life and to realize how precious life is and how important it is for us to live it to the fullest.

***

As I started to review my experiences and things that happened to my life, I think that I need to pass them on to others to know about them so that they can learn from my mistakes. The younger students can learn something to help themselves in their life-long learning and knowing things that I have been through with different cultures, different countries so it can be beneficial and help them. I was almost dead and was almost not able to be together with my parents and grow up. I was able to pass all the hard courses when I was a countryside student, which enabled me to pass my high school classes. My life turned to a different path when I left Vietnam at the age of 18. I went to several US schools and finished. However, there was one degree that I did not finish. I received a couple of bachelor degrees, master and double PhDs. I have also had many turns on the path of my life such as my family falling apart. I lost lots of money in real estate during the economic Great Recession in 2006. I lost my first job after complete my PhD. But I was able to go through these trials and experienced so many things that I never experienced before. I have been through these tough times and good times, and through reading this I hope the reader will gain some benefit and look at some of my experiences that I went through as an examples to view things in life so it can help the reader in their life-long learning.

I also feel that learning is the life-long experience and processes to continue develop and improve ourselves. No matter what stage of life one is in, we still can learn something, even from a book or from someone else's experiences.

***

Throughout my life, I also have so many questions to ask myself. When I was young, I normally asked questions about nature and science around us such as, "Why is the sky blue? Why do we need to drink? Why do we need oxygen to breath?" The list goes on and on. When I got older, I started to think about my life and started to ask myself, "What have I accomplished so far in my life? What do I want to do next? What is the most important thing in life? What is most important at this stage of my life? What do I want to accomplish next? What have I learned and experienced from my own life story/experience and others? What will I do differently?" And, "What will others benefit from my own life experience?" The list goes on and on. As I asked more and more questions about myself, I started to review and understand myself more. When I understood myself more, I was able to know what I needed to do next, how and what I need to do to accomplish it.

As we grow older in life, we tend to forget and lose focus on our long-time goal, the goal that we set when we are young. So, we need to keep up ourselves and find the way to help us motivate ourselves. Sometimes the reason to motivate ourselves could be the loved ones in our family or friends. Most of the time, we need to have friends and people to share our things and people to expression ourselves to, people who understand us, who can communicate with us and who we can talk to. But I learned that depend on each stage of our life; friends and the person that we can talk to will be different, but we really need to have people to talk to whether it is a significant other or the loved one is in our family or a friend.

***

Writing is also a very interesting experience. It is not like before. I used to write science papers and dissertation, but this time I am writing out the chapters of my life. I feel each stage in my life is an adventure with so many interesting events and I am excited to share them with you, the reader.

As a little child, we may not know much about why we need to go to school, the benefit of going to school, and how we can prepared for it unless our parents explain to us. And how much money our parents spend for our school. But today, the cost of going to school is expensive. School is an investment; we need to choose wisely. Why do we need to go to college? A four-year and higher college degree does not guarantee our stable income in the future but at least it gives us more opportunity and more chances and prepares us for opportunities. We go to school with so much money to pay for tuition and living expenses. As an example of myself, I spent much time in school and ended up borrowing much from loans for my school expenses. I experienced many things and learned the lesson that, it is easy to borrow, but it is very hard to pay it back. So we need to manage well, otherwise we will end up with a lot of debts.

There are so many thing that I didn't learn in school. School does not give you real life experience. School only prepares you for reading, writing, and the ability to comprehend things and the ability to learn. School did not teach us how to handle problems and manage money well. This you need to learn by yourself or through life experience.

Therefore, it is very hard for each of us to know how to prepare when the tough time came and we need to look back at ourselves and our own pathway or our own direction that we have been down thus far.

If we just continue our behavior and do things that are not great or negative things over and over, they could become negative habits. The habits of never looking back and never realizing that you have gone so far and improved and prepared yourself if you are having a good day or bad day, makes it harder to recognize if we did something wrong or did something not great for our benefit. When I was young, I did not realize this, not until later during the economic recession when things got tougher and harder. So, we need to pick a path or direction that not only fulfills our own desires, but also fills our need and also brings us peace.

I constantly thought about how to handle problems in life, but it always turned out in the way that I did not want in family, relationships, and work. We do not want to change but it is happening and it is the thing that needs to be in order for us to move into the next stage.

1

My Childhood and The Memory That I Will Never Forget

Every one of us all has a childhood, whether good or bad, and it is full of memories. We all remember life as a little child with peaceful times of life. Our life is so peaceful because we only live for the current moment, so do not think much about our future and past. But as the little child, we all were dependent on our parents and their life experience.

My childhood story is not common like other children. Instead of daily activities full of toys, I only had a few toys. And all these toys I played with, I had to make by myself. In a Third World country back in 1980, there are not many things available to obtain, to sell, and we also were not able to afford much.

I made a kite by using bamboo frame and our recycled papers or used notebook papers from school. I had to use whatever was available as materials to make these toys. I also made a yo-yo to play with friends. However, with these toys, I had so much fun, full of joy and friends around me. We normally gathered in the neighbor's house and played these games. These toys and the daily activities kept me full of peace and full of happiness. I really enjoyed each of these games. To this day, I still remember when we gathered together. I really missed these times and my childhood in Vietnam. So, no matter how poor or rich our family is, we still can have and deserve a happy and peaceful childhood.

My childhood was also full of peaceful times and memories with the grass field and rice field. When the harvest season came, we gathered with Dad's friends and we celebrated and had a great dinner after the harvest. We worked together and had a great time. Even though it was very hard work, we manage to work together and share the fun. And share the joy. At the age of 12 years old and younger, I already started to work in the coffee field on the farm to help my Dad.

The Day I Was Born

I was born and raised in Lam Dong, Viet Nam. I left Viet Nam and came to the U.S.A. as a refugee at the age of 18. I was born in the family with both of my parents and I have my grandparents who really love me. However, I went through a lot of suffering because of the war. But our parents and grandparents teach us to value the culture and traditions from our ancestors. I was raised with such care and full of love with family members surrounding me. We were raised with a culture and tradition from our ancestors, with high values and respect for our elderly parents and grandparents.

There is a familiar folk poem in the traditional six-eight style known to every Vietnamese person since the very first days knew how to speak. Our traditions set priority on respecting our parents and the elderly; our parents teach us to value the elderly as young children. My parent and grandmother often recite the poem to me.

"Công cha như núi Thái sơn
Nghĩa mẹ như nước trong nguồn chảy ra
Một lòng thờ mẹ kính cha
Cho tròn chữ hiếu mới là đạo con"

A rough translation of the poem is
"Merits of father are like the Thai mountain[1]

---

[1] Thai mountain is unimaginably high, just like all the merits and hard-works a father does to his child

Good deep of the mother are like water running from
the source[2]
Whole-heartedly revere mother and respect father
Fully fulfilling the word of piety, that's a child's
obligation."

Unlike most of the kids the same age as me, they went through a normal life but my life was much different. When I was born my Dad was in the communist camp and he stayed there for seven years after that. I was born and raised with a typical Vietnamese mindset with hard work and a belief in hard work. Listen and respect the elderly. My Mom was mainly responsible for raising me and my two other older brothers and older sister.

From the time to time my mother carried me with food to visit my Dad. I remember my Mom and Dad used to tell me that when I was about one year old, my Mom carried me to visit my Dad. I pointed my hand to my Dad and asked Mom, "Who is this man?" So there is not much time my Dad was around me until I was eight years old. So definitely, I was closed to Mom than my Dad. However, my Dad also inspired me with his life and many of the great stories from the camp that he went through.

We had to obey well all my parents' rules. As a young kid, I already obeyed my parents' rules very well. I listened and did the things my parents said and sometimes without a thought. However, when I grew up, sometimes I felt like there were warning signs and I was forced to do and think that, but it might not be the best way. But time went by, when I was old enough and went through a lot of experiences and suffering, I realized that my parents were right and the entire thing that he/she

---

[2] Water from the source runs endlessly, just like the love and will of a mother for her child is perpetual and forever-lasting

warned was what they already went through, a great suffering and have learned a great deal in life in order to achieve and obtain these, and learn the lesson. This is why they seemed demanding from time to time but I realized that sometimes they force us to do things only for our own good that they think is for our own good.

Our foundation was based on the respect of the elderly and built from our family down. We were also taught not to look directly at the elderly's eye when we talk to them. This is a sign of disrespect.

You only have this life

We only have one time to live in this life, we need to value it, do the thing that we want to do, make it meaningful and enjoyable.

Do we have our own destiny when we are born? We need to fulfill our own needs and desires. Every one of us knows that we were born, and one day we will leave this world. We do not know when but that is our destination. We need to do such thing that we will not regret in each stage of our life. In each stage of our life, there are challenges, but if we endure them, they make us stronger and stronger.

Buda also said that we are born with our own destination. If we want to change our destination, we first need to accept it. We need to accept that we were born, grew up, and one day we will get old, and one day we will leave this world. If we are born and complete our destination, achieve our goal, we have completed our own destination in this life; we complete our purpose of life. For those who completed their destination when they left this world, they were eternally happy.

Our life in this world is not permanent and not forever. After we come into this world, we may live for ten years, possibly a hundred years, or perhaps even longer. But we grow, and finally we have to die. So we have to value our life, live our live in a way that is meaningful, not only for our own benefit but also for people around us and for this world.

2

My Simple Childhood But So Peaceful

The way we live our life is also affected by and depends upon our own parent, who teach us how to live and their general perspective in life and experience.

My daily activities were school in the morning, help my parents in the afternoon, and do homework and study during the nighttime. There is the time that I had to rise and feed our cows and water buffalos. I like them very much. This did not happen until I was in middle school, in sixth through eighth grades. We needed to raise cows to obtain manure for fertilization of our coffee. Most the time, I led our cows and water buffalo to a place away from home for them to eat grass and hay. Each end of the day, I tried to bring back home hay by carrying it on the trailer or hanging it on the back of the cows. This hay will be used to feed cows in the later season, rainy days, or bad weather days. It was hard work and very difficult because there was not much equipment so I had to tie hay to carry it home. There was not so much hay available. I normally asked people and worked hard looking for it. I also led a water buffalo to bring home wood for us to cook. To do this, it normally took me almost the whole day long to look for wood and to let the water buffalo pull it home by the trailer or by cart.

Boy riding water buffalo while playing flute

Kite flying (kite that make music) in summer time

Rice field in Da Lat, Lam Dong, near where I
used to live when I was in VietNam

We consider ourselves farmers and a middle class family back in 1980. But our live is very hard. We had houses and properties, but we needed to raise coffee, rice, and other vegetables to feed our own. I remember the days that we sold most of our coffee to people to get food. We basically sold coffee for food and our living expenses. So our living depended much on the things we grew and the successfulness of the season. Sometimes, we did not have much to reserve for next year. For several years after the Vietnam war, we did not have much rice and coffee to reserve for the next year. But things started to pick up better when I got older. Much later, I learned we needed to reserve for the rainy day. That idea, I did not experience and learned much until later in life.

Studying at nighttime with Mom

The little cowboy "Cậu Bé Chăn Trâu" now is grown up. Time flew by, even though our life is very much not full of treasures, but I feel it was very peaceful. This is one of the lessons that I feel is important; sometimes you do not need a life full of material thing to be happy and have a peaceful life. Even much later, my live in the US is full of material possessions but I still do not feel as happy as I was when I was little. So, the inner peace and the childhood life and peaceful time and memories were carried throughout my life.

My life is full of great memories. I remember that I received an award for being a good student when I was in the first grade and up. I don't remember much from when I was in first and second grade, but one of the most memorable events was when I received an award and walked home with a very happy face to show to my Mom and my grandmother. I remember the feeling of accomplishment and joy. To reward me, my Mom and my grandmother give me a banana. That is what they had, but it made me really happy for the caring and appreciate for my accomplishment.

Grandmother used to sell bananas to people. She had a small grocery shop to sell things to people, and later my Mom also did that and she had her own. My grandmother was close to me when I was little and even when she passed away, my brother Max and I were there.

Banian tree in town, picture was taken in once of the town in Ha-Noi, VietNam

Besides the close interaction with Mom and my grandmother, in my childhood I was also close to the banian tree in our town. My childhood also relates to our own town banana tree "Cây đa đầu làng." It is connected to my early childhood. The banian tree in our town is really big and it is next to our middle school. We normally sit on it's roof and tried to pick the baby leaves to eat. These baby leaves had a sour taste. But sometimes it is also brought scary memories to me as I was a child because most of the elders said there were a lot of scary things that happened during the nighttime such as ghosts. I never wanted to be out there in the dark during the nighttime. I learned much later that this scare story from the elder was only to keep us safe and prevent us from going out during the nighttime.

3

Growing Up and Education

We are not grown up if we have never been suffering or been through tragedy. We learn and value much in life after these suffering and tragedy. We also learn much when we travel and spend time with people around us and share our story, our suffering.

From time to time, I remember those days when I was a little boy. Much later, I went to high school. My hometown does not have high school, so we had to go to school far away from home. It is over 20 km (about 12.5 miles) away. We basically biked and stayed there and came back home each week. We stayed in my friend's brother's house.

We stayed together and cooked and ate together. It was so much joy and sharing. We all grew up together. We tried to live as close to each other as possible. We lived in one of our friend's brother's house, Doan, for the first few moths when we started high school.

There was no dorm so we had to cook and prepare food on our own. It was very hard work to prepare food and cook for all of us.

We were able to stay together for a while, but my friend's brother was not happy because there were seven of us living in that house. However, we were so happy. We were able to live there for a couple of weeks and my friend's brother asked us to leave. We were able to move to a different place right after that. But Doan still stayed there because it was his brother's house. Later, he asked us, "Why did you ask Huy to stay with you?" His brother asked him, Doan told me. Because we feel that we were not so happy so all us left the house and moved to another place. But I already left and Doan felt so sad that he was not able to keep me. His brother told him that I was a good student, and if I stayed with him I could help him to study. Sadly, Doan was only able to study for few moths and could not keep up with the studies so he quit the school.

There was much work, effort, and discipline to keep up with at school and we were always studying at home once we were just in the ninth grade. We also had to cook and feed ourselves. But we had to buy food and prepare the meals for us each day. Each day after school, we needed to go buy grocery and things to prepare for the meal. We were so hungry after each day when school was over. There was only half day school, but we did not get back until late afternoon. I remember a lot of times, we did not even have enough charcoal for us to cook but we used whatever was available and managed through it. So basically our live were very independent and we had to prepare on our own. But we also did not have much money. Each week we received some money and rice from our parents. However, because we were new to the area and had to study, none of us were able to find any work or earn any money to support ourselves yet.

This happened to all of us. We had to depend on the money we received from our parents. But there was not much extra so we could only live for the week. Each week, our parents gave us rice and a little money to buy food for a week. Most of the time, we had to eat rice with fish sauce or with soy sauce. We could not buy bread because it was too expensive. So it was very hard to live for us but we had the great experience and we were very dedicated. We helped each other to study. Besides six of us lived together and there were several others who did not live together with us. But the bad thing is that all the others could not make it to tenth grade and I am the only one that made into passed grade nine to grade ten. I was so sad that all of my friends in my group were going back to my town and only I studied in grade ten. I was able to continue on to the eleventh grade and finish, starting twelfth grade before I went to the US.

Hard work and dedication pay off. But most of us were missing some trigonometry math knowledge. We also had many disadvantages as we had studied in the countryside, compared to the city, because most people in the city were prepared and went to summer school and learned things and were much better prepared before us. We did not have much chance and advantage. Most of us were missing most of the basics and could not compete with student in the city, not because they were smart but because of the way we prepared and the materials and the level of competition. We were not quite prepared enough for but I studied hard and was able to pass my courses.

The exams to get into high school, ninth grade, were also a challenge. I remember, we had to study hard for the exam. One day, my friends and I stayed late to study and sleep in one of our house. We had two houses next each other. We also went on and tried to feed ourselves with whole chicken that night. Back there, a whole chicken was very expensive for us and we could not afford it. We only had whole chicken during New Years or on special occasions. But we did eat a whole chicken that night.

We also tried to eat my Dad's bananas during our study nights. This only happens on our group study night. My study friends were Thuy, Vinh and Doan. "We should try to study," I said. We went over chapter after chapter. We normally fell into sleep after three to five hours. We all so tried and could not do any more studying. We normally needed to burn a candle and oil flame for our studying. Back there, there is no electricity in our town yet.

4

My First Impression and Views About the U.S.A.

Sometimes, we all think that, we can do such amazing thing but then realize that we are also human. There are things that could not turn out the way we like, but it gives us a chance to see different thing that happen and we live life better and we become stronger and stronger.

Simple and easy life helps us to stay more focused on ourselves. And this helps us to be less distract. Thus, creating and improving our enjoyment and happiness.

The US tradition teaches us to become more independent at a much earlier stage than the Asian culture.

View of downtown Seattle from Alki Beach, Seattle, WA

UW Seattle campus on the rainy day

We were on an airplane traveling from Vietnam to Thailand, then to Japan and then to USA. My older brother had already escaped Vietnam when he was 12. He sent us money a few times and let us know how his life was in the US. He was adopted by a few different families until he turned 18 years old. He sent us pictures of him and his adopted Dad was in a private airplane, I felt very happy for him and I thought that it was a fulfillment of happiness. Because he can enjoy the freedom and do thing in US as he like.

My impression of the US was as a heaven. But it was different when I saw it. Sure it was a lot of change, and much better than our country, but we had to work hard to adapt to it because it was much different than Vietnam. I learned that life in America has so much opportunity and it is better in terms of clean air and freedom, but it also has some negatives in term of traditional culture. The traditional Vietnam culture teaches us that we care and be around parents more even as we grow up. But I learn that is not typical of children in the US. They only live with their parents until they are 18 years old and then they go to college and live by themselves. Even if some do not go to college, the majority of them do not live with parents. The US teaches us not to be so dependent upon our parents. We experiment and learn things and even fall down but we still need to step up by ourselves. The parents help but the culture teaches us more independence. Unlike our Vietnamese and most traditional Asian culture, where we were guarded and overseen by our parents. This happened when the child was just born and started to learn how to walk. There are times that we fall when we learn how to walk, but our parent will likely hold on to us and oversee. Unlike the western tradition where you will be on your own and it is less likely to see the parents try to hold the child. The child is more independent and responsible and freely experiences thing by themselves.

American flag with Statue of Liberty

Throughout life, I am seeking the knowledge that our parents try to pass on to us. It is so great and I should appreciate it. Most of the experiences that they went through in life are through hard work and devastation, and with a lot of suffering, so it is great to listen to the elders and learn from them. The western culture also teaches us how to listen and be our own person. The western culture teaches us to be independent and be ourselves more than Asian traditional beliefs and cultures. This is great in a sense that once we are ready, we need to experience and seek things happening around us and learn from our own mistakes. This very great in some sense because the western culture tries to teach the kids to be independent and be responsible for what we have done even we are little. However, the Vietnamese tradition also teaches the child be independent and responsible for the things in their life. but it is guarded and guided by parents. Once the children are old enough, then they likely let them do the things on their own and be independent. This is great, but the Asian culture prevents the child from experiencing things around them and how to learn and respond to their mistakes. The world is so dynamic, such as the way that it is changing everyday. So it is both great and bad because young people have the opportunity to have experiences during the process of learning to become independent, so it takes longer to achieve. The western culture is much more responsible and is independent much earlier than the Asian culture. The Asian culture is also good in some sense but most of the time Asian child can stay longer with parents and depend on the parents. This is bad in some perspectives because it may affect the connection, interaction, and appreciate from the parents. The Asian culture would diminish our chance of interactive with the environment or slow down the time to interact with grown ups and increase our age to become independent. But this may be good in some respect because our parents do not want anything bad to happen to their own child. This is not only good, but all the parents want their child to be good and safe, to be a good person, to have some positive impact on the world, and a good impact on the environment and things surrounding us. But eventually they have to let children be themselves.

"You know that there is so much freedom in America?" My older brother commented. The US has freedom of speech and freedom to bare arm. I remember that back there we cannot even tell the true story about things that happened and what happened to us in the very early days in Vietnam after Vietnam War. But we only focus on fulfilling our basic needs, such as food and materials needed for our own daily life. But we can visit and talk to our neighbors and friends more frequently than the US tradition.

***

Tulip field in Washington

"How come I cannot talk to our neighbor?" I asked my older brother.

"That is their private property. We need to obey theirs and cannot run to their properties unless we ask," my older brother answered. Surely this is true. Whenever we dropped something, such as ball, we need to ask for permission to enter their backyard to pick it up. People are more independent in their private properties and by themselves than traditional culture in Vietnam. We see that each family has their own privacy and they are separated by fences from each other's. Each family interacts with and is more open to neighbors with less privacy and each house in Vietnam is more exposed to the neighbor. The houses are also more open and next to each other. This is the only effect of the culture of Vietnam that we all share and people talk to each other more often (people talk to their neighbor more than in the US).

The Vietnamese idioms that represent this case is; "Better a neighbor near than a brother far off." The neighborhood is very useful and necessary in case of emergencies.

Western culture teaches us that we do not talking about others. We try to improve by taking care of things that are our own responsibility. This is surely the true process. I still remember up to this day that our neighbors had a big truck and a lot of time it was not running. We could help by pulling and letting the engine start. People are willing to help. I also see this happen a lot in US. People are helping people and taking care of those who are poorer than us. I seek that people will want to help and really care for the poor, especially those that are in the mission and help everyone of us whenever they are needed.

The Asian culture also prevents our own self-development because some of the parents and grandparents really love their children and keep them under their wing and prevent them from having a chance to be more independent. Because they believe that they should keep their children under their wing so they can protect them from whatever things happened in life. But I learned much later that, in a relationship, it is hard for a husband or a wife to be away from their parents because they want to protect themselves even when their child is old enough and married and has their own family. They support that their children want to be independent and build their family, but sometimes the traditional still want to keep a close relationship with them. So there is a good and bad sign in Asian culture and also good and bad in western culture. In western culture, sometimes the parents give them too much freedom and they do too much on their own and things can go away from their parents attention, especially with the high technology. This makes it very difficult for parents to guard their children. Because the technology comes out daily and we have to catch up with these technologies. Technology supports and serves us but there is so much information, and parents are not able to guide and guard their child.

"Can you get on Facebook to teach Thi and guide her to study for her school?" said my older brother. This thing can happen from time-to-time and it is hard to control because the child can be exposed to things on the internet and information that they are not supposed to read as their age. So as more technology develops and is used in our daily life, our parents need to keep up with it. This is very hard for busy parents and for parents that are away from their child.

One time I went and visited my older brother family. Each of the member in the family all have their own iPad and use it to look up things on the internet and watch movies and do things on their own. So less communication, less interactivity, and less time together between each individual member in the house. This is what is suffered in the western culture and technology pulls people away from each other and gives us less time to spend and communicate as there used to be. The more time we spend together, the more we understand and improve our relationship. Technology isolates us and keeps us in our own space and our own area. We can call this as the virtual life and is so much different than our own normal life. Each message and text could affect our emotions. We spend lots of time in search and text and chatting to people away from us. And our emotions and the way we express ourselves is different than our real life. We end up emotionally affected by the messages and texts from friends and people around the world, the virtual world. The internet and technology should be a good way to communicate and express ideas to serve us. So we need to realize it has a good and bad effect on us. The internet and technology should support to serve us in a good way of communicating and expressing ourselves, but we tend to isolate ourselves and stay in our virtual world. Parents need to teach the child, be by their side and be together with them in every step, when they are exposed to the internet and new technology.

I also realized that we do not spend much time and eat dinner and meals together like we used to do as time goes by. This is because each of us gets too busy with school and work, but we spend time together in the church and family meals as much as we can. We cannot blame it on being busy because we do not have time but because each of us just isolates ourselves in our own in virtual world and our own domain. We need to understand, open up, and communicate with our own family members and seek things that happened to each of us and other members of our own family.

5

The Process for the HO Paperwork

The gate has some meaning and it is the process by which we separate different types of people. But only you know if and how to turn it to the great and joyful.

The process for finishing the paperwork to go to the US was difficult and we waited for several years. My Dad had to finish all the paperwork. The program that brought us to the US was called Humanitarian Operation (HO). It served as the refuge program for people from South Vietnam during the Vietnam War. Humanitarian Program for Former Political Detainees, popularly called Humanitarian Operation or HO due to the "H" subgroup designation within the ODP (e.g. H01-H09, H10, etc.). The program was set up to benefit former South Vietnamese who were involved in the former regime or worked for the US and allowed to immigrate to the US if they had suffered persecution by the communist regime after 1975.

There is so much effect left behind after the war. Our house that Dad used a lot of golds to build in 1974 in the expensive lot and is next to the main market in the province, was bombed down during the war. But the odd thing is that, our house is the only house that was bombed and destroyed. We were not able to rebuild and live in the house. We then moved close to my grandmother and stayed close to my grandmother and my grandfather. Our family is not the same as before. The end of the war was the cause of our house to burn down and it affected our family greatly. These changes cost us too much. We were suffering after the war but luckily our family was still reunited after almost eight years without my Dad. That is so much of the effect and changes with our lives. Thing were so much different from the war. *Sitting in the airplane thinking back on what we had been through, I was terrifying myself, but I felt so proud that we had been through so much and our family was still together, my parents still alive.*

Now I am in the airplane and we are traveling to another country, to the U.S.A, the country that we think should have more opportunities and freedom. It is so great that we have the opportunity. Sometimes we do not know what will happen in the future but at least we live for the moment and pay the price for it. We were trying hard to keep everybody safe. We always believe that we will be better and better with each day.

Our airplane stopped at Thailand Airport and we were transferred to a waiting area. I already saw many different things than in Vietnam. We waited for a few hour and we then boarded to travel to Japan by American Airline. Another airplane took us to Japan where we waited about six hours in the Japan Airport. I already started seeing more changes. And this is the third time I was in the airport. Besides the one in Vietnam Airport, Thailand airport and now I was in one of the airports in Japan.

This trip is the first ever that we were on an airplane. I see so much change in the airport and things that I never see, like cars to carry and transport luggage, which all work by machine and are well organized. I did not see this kind of thing before.

We then boarded the American airplane to travel to the U.S.A. We arrived at Tacoma SeaTac Airport. My grandmother, our relatives, aunt and my uncle were already waiting for us in the airport. We are so happy. The thing that we saw in the airport was so much better. The first impression I had was that it was so great to see our uncles, aunt, my relatives, and grandmother. We cried tears of happiness for the reunion after being apart for so many years, now we can see each other again.

I was in my uncle's car that took us to our apartment. My brother rented us an apartment. It took a while to go out from the airport and out to the parking lot. The parking lot building in the airport was so high with so many cars. I later learned that the average car per person in the city that I was living in is 1.5 cars per person. My impression of the freeway was how big it is and with many lanes and roads that connected to each other. This is also the first time I was in a private car. We do not have cars in Vietnam. So I already observed and saw much different things than Vietnam.

We finally arrived to our new place 15 minutes after that. We then gathered at our uncle's house an hour later to celebrate. My uncle prepared the celebration for us. We were so happy and we ate a lot of food. It is so great to see my relatives and this is the first time that I was at a party with so many of my family members and our relatives. I was so happy to see each and every one of them. They are so happy to see us and happy for us. We were gathering and we were all so happy. It was a moment of joyful happiness in our lifes, the joy and happiness for being together again after so many years away from each other.

***

I was in the school for people who first come to U.S.A. and in the transition to the permanent school. The name of my first high school was Sharpless High School. At Sharpless High School, things were already different. I was woken up and caught the bus at 6:45am and the classes started at 7:45am. The bus took me directly to my school. "Good morning," said the bus driver.

"Good morning," I replied. I felt like people are so polite and friendly. This is the common way to say hello. I really feel happy and like it because I do not have to take a bike to school as I did in Vietnam. After several pick ups, the bus dropped us in front of Sharpless High School. We then went to eat breakfast. The first impression was that the meal was already prepared and the service was so nice and clean. I lined up to pick up my cake and milk and sat down at the table to eat. Things were so different. The buildings were clean and nice. The landscapes were nice as well. Things are so great for us. Tables and chairs were so clean and well organized, well arranged. The whole school was so clean and nicely painted as I observed. I was impressed with the clean and nice school, which was well organized and with people so politely, and I felt that it was much better than my high school in Vietnam.

We then entered English class. We also took math, PE, and history courses. But our main focus was on English and the preparation for my other permanent school where I could go and be around my relatives there.

"This is the Mercedes," said my classmate. We were sitting on the bus on our way home. I never saw this car before. I did not even recognize it and noticed the difference until years later. I see the start in a circle logo but they are the same with any other cars. I could not notice the difference in logos. The only thing I observed is I see the car and how people use it for their transportation. The living standard here was so high. People are traveling by cars. This is one of the reasons why the US consumes the most gasoline in the world.

"Do you know how to drive a car?" I asked my classmate.

"I will try to learn it later," he replied.

"I need to save and go to work to buy a car," I said. This did not happen until much later when I went to Chief Sealth High School after six moths. The school was named after a native U.S.A. Indian Sealth and Chief who was the head of the group in the Indian province.

I saw and met different types of people in the school, people from Vietnam, people from Africa, Somalia and so on. I never saw this many different types of people before. Their culture was different as well. I was taught when I was little that when speaking and talking, we cannot look into the eyes of the elderly. This is not polite. Unlike in US, we teach that we have to focus and make eye contact. When talking to people eye contact is a good way of communication and focusing.

Communication through eye and body langue is important and a good way to express your ideas throughout. People are told to listen and pay attention to you as well when we are able to combine both body expression and word.

I feel people are so polite and volunteer to obey the rules and respect others well. There is waiting in line whenever we go to lunch, even with the teacher or the principle of the school. Everyone is equal when we eat. There is no cutting in line for trying to please others. Unlike the Asian culture where we focus on the boss, but here we treat everyone equally.

In the first few moths, my daily activities were so easy for me because I had so much time to study and do homework. Each day, I woke up around 6:30am, catch the bus, and go to school. I took the same bus home and did homework at home. We did not have school on Saturday and Sunday. My daily schedule did not fill up with much activity yet. After a couple months, I felt I mastered and did well in school because I was mainly forced to learn English. I also did so well in calculus and U.S. history. I was selected as the good student with the highest grade in the calculus course that I took. The principle took a picture of me and posted on the school wall.

"Do not listen to Vietnamese music but listen to other people talking, even at the bus or when you are walking. You will learn some new vocabulary and new things," said the English teacher. I also agreed that it was a good way to pick up vocabulary and the pronunciation when people talk and it made it easy to view the world and see how others pronounce words when people were talking.

The school seemed very easy for me. My daily schedule started with picking up things like going to visit and talk to my relatives so I can adjust my self with new environments, babysitting, and playing with my younger relatives when I have time while visiting my grandmother.

I also learned that family meals and family gatherings are very important. This is because it is a good way that we can communicate and understand our daily activities from one to other members of the family. The dinner meal is our daily activity for us to meet and see our family members. My daily activities started to pickup even more after my older brother started to delivery newspapers. Three afternoons each week, I started to pick up and deliver papers with my older brother. He is still in college at that time. He and I really enjoyed the work. We looked at the address and followed my brother's directions. I was able to delivery newspapers. This was my first job in the U.S. My work started to pick up even more and in the next following week I was able to pick up newspapers and deliver on my own. This is not very hard. I started to see different houses and know people. I was able to start a short conversation and said hello to people and pedestrians whenever I passed by.

My older sister started to work in the bakery company during the weekend. I followed her and she was also able to get me a job for the weekend as well. The pastry work at the bakery was only done during the weekend and I started to earn more money. Within one-and-a-half years later, I was able to save enough money to buy a used car. The cost of the used Honda was $4000.

I was able to pass my written exam very quickly. I obtained my instructional permit and started to practice my driving with my older brother. I was so happy to learn and practice car driving with my older brother. We first needed to pass the instructional permit exam. Then, after passing the driving, we would get the drivers license. The instructional permit is the written test. The law requires that only people who have drivers licenses and have driven for more than five years were able to teach, sit in the car, and give instruction to people who just have the instructional permit. My brother left Vietnam when he was twelve. He obtained his drivers license more than five years later. He lent me his Mitsubishi and he taught me how to drive. He drove me to a place with less people or the cemetery.

"You should pray to these who passed away there in the cemetery so they will help you learn how to drive quickly and faster," said my Dad.

It did not take too much time for me to practice driving. After several weeks of practice, I was able to pass my driven test.

"Please go ahead," said the driving examiner after entering and sitting in the car. I was buckled in and turned on the engine and drove, as he instructed me where to go. I drove and he asked me to parallel park, backup, and park around the corner. I was able to do well and got a passing score. I was so happy that I was able to hold my drivers license that I may not able to obtain if I was in Vietnam. The car helps us to have lot of freedom to go when and wherever we want go. But we need to know where to go first. We need our start and finial destination. This is what I realized much later in life. If we know where to go in life and our final destination we can get there. But our life is like an adventure. It is exploring and finding out things that we do not know and things that we never experienced. Each level of experiment and achievement is different. Truly, life is an adventure, and we may not know back there that we will be in the US someday and now almost 25 years have gone by.

***

The college here is great and fun. I have so many great times with new friends in South Seattle Community College (SSCC).

"Hit that ball and here is the ball," said my friend at SSCC. I started to go to college to take courses when I was in my senior year at Chief Sealth High School almost a year after I arrived in the US. Truly, we need to interact and connect to people around us. The energy and things around us give us much experience and valuable lessons to learn to adapt. Our human mind has the capability to adapt to and to fit well to new environments and new cultures.

While in high school, I also worked after school at Fred Hutchinson Cancer Research Center (FHCRC). FHCRC is one of the worlds biggest and number one to do cancer research and provide methods for curing cancer. They now also have a hospital as well. I first started working after school in the work training program and was hired as part-time as a lab aid and then a lab worker. I normally worked after school and weekends to prepare glassware and to do culture tissues, preparing media and culture for cells. Sometime, I also did quality control as well. Sometime, it popped up in my mind, that if I continue with chemistry, then I would end up continuing to work there.

***

With great records from high school in Vietnam and my great scores at Chief Sealth High School and from the Running Start Program at SSCC, I got accepted to the University of Washington. My relative that went to Chief Sealth High School did not go to UW but went to community college and finished Associate of Arts degrees there. UW was a sign of showing a great effort and accomplishment on my part to demonstrate that I was able to go to a four-year university and catch up with my studies and life in the US. UW was also a very good school that many people could not get accepted to. My parents were so happy for me because I could attend a four-year university, and it is a great school where I was able to learn to help myself in the future.

Sitting down at my desk, I still could not really believe that we were already in the US for almost two years and I had started UW for my first year with many expectations. I wrote and picking up things that I could use to prepare myself with the mindset that I would able to do well in school. Surely, I would be able to attend UW and finish my two bachelors degrees within four years and one-quarter. I started to take the graduate courses when I was in my senior year.

Sometimes you will not be able to feel and see it and know what it looks like until you go through it. The feeling and experience is amazing. The amazing thing is that your can accomplish something that you have never done before. The two bachelor's degrees also created a problem for me later on because it led me to two different paths. One degree is related to medical and the other is an engineering degree. This is also helping me to fulfill the requirement to enter medical school later on.

6

Education in U.S.A.: The Interaction with a New Culture and Adapting to a New Culture

Each of us all learns something new in the different stages of our life and become adapted to it. This new adaptation and new change are another opportunity and joy once we are ready, open to it, and accept it.

Through out my life, I have met a lot of people and experienced them entering my life and leaving me with something and with some footprints. Ms. Alavesa asked me to come to her house to eat with her and her student. Ms. Alavesa was my Chief Sealth High School teacher and she had much impact on me and inspired my writing. She taught me English. The open house was a way to introduce people to view a house that was for sale and to market the house, but I was think that it is it a way that people try to know each other and open their house to the neighbors to introduce themselves. I did not know it until later that it is the way the agent wants people to view and see the house. But I used it as an example to explain how people can get together to know each other and used it for the essay in Ms. Alevasa class. I know that even when we make a mistake you still can learn and improve in the process. Ms. Alevasa helped me to improve myself and my writing during my time in high school. She was my inspiration in the way she taught and kept the focus and even though I made a mistake, I still learned something new.

My inspiration changed from time to time. At UW, my inspiration was Professor Smith with self-improving and inspiration for higher education and to go to graduate school. From time to time, Prof. Smith guided me in school and worked with me for my engineering senior project. Along our life, we need to have people that can inspire us and

31

to help us so we can motivate ourselves. And this person can change from time to time and in the different stages of our life.

As a little child, my culture taught me that I was imprisoned by my parents on their discipline and they would consistently raise me and be there with me through out my life, through band things and great things.

We had learned that we needed to share and care for each member of the family. We also needed to care for people around us. One of the great images that I still keep in my mind when I was student in Vietnam is, while biking, the Vietnamese teacher stopped to pick up the tree branches on the street when she saw them because it may effect others and create accidents or damage to others. I remember the great image of picking up the tree branches on the street, showing the way that we need to do it and to care for others because it can effect us and impact others around us. And it is good for our living condition our environment. We need to improve our roads and improve our environment, improve out living conditions but each of us has responsible for it.

***

I was different than you, so you can hate me and beat me. Some people see others differently and if he or she did not do things the way or the same as they insisted or want, then they can beat us. Tri and other polices that work for his Dad try to stop and beat me on my way biking back to my home from school back there when I was in Vietnam in grade 10. When it happened, a lot of people and pedestrians saw it, so they ran to and try to stop him from trying to beat me. That image and memory went through my life. I still remember it from time to time and see that people feel annoyed and easily get mad sometimes if they see the way you act differently than their expectation.

My Dad was called up to the principal's office to find out what happened. This is not a great thing because I did not do anything wrong, and he saw that I was different, that I came from a little town so that he can beat me. I feel very ashamed for him with the way he treats me. This is not the way it should happen. I was a polite kid but did not try to make him angry.

I feel very sad because of this situation. My Dad was called in and he was calmed by the principal. Everyone knew what happen. I never beat him or did any bad thing to him but only because I was different. I came from the little town with the different accent.

This thing is very similar. I was traveling back to my Dad's town but because of my different tone of speaking, they are trying to beat me as well. *They do not understand the difference and open their heart to it. They only think of themselves.* They lay blame and say that, because you are different, I don't like it and do not want to have a peaceful relationship or interaction. This is what I learned; we need to accept the differences. Each of us is already different than others in everything. Each of us is unique and there is none identical in both physical and personality. This is what we have to do: accept it and live with it. No one is the same as anyone else. *Culture, religion, physical, and personality are always different in each and every one of us. This is what I learned from experience, and I see that, in order to have a peaceful relationship, we need to appreciate it and accept all the differences.*

Our view of and thoughts about things around us change from time to time. The most common thought is we normally fulfill our most basic needs. Once our basic needs are fulfilled, such as food, materials (such as car, transportation, and so on), we tend to fulfill our mental needs. So we need not only full fill our basic daily consuming, like food and drink for our body's need but also spiritual needs. *The normal people are work hard to fulfill the basic needs; food, house, and materials. And once these basic needs are fulfilled we tend to focus on our mental and spiritual.*

7

My Mother Has Inspired Me and Led Me for Most of My Respond

Each of us all have people that inspired and motivated us through different stage of our life.

My Mom has been so much inspiration to me since I was a little child. I know that every one of us is not perfect, but my Mom is so great in the way she takes care of us and leads our family.

I talk to Dr. Wang and feel the emotion about my childhood life.

The high-speed train heading to Tainan, Taiwan from Taipei. "I was told by Mom and Dad that, because my Mom was paralyzed after giving birth to me, she could not get up or even take care of herself. So basically, all the doctors at the hospital suggested that my Mom should give me to someone else to raise and to take care of me." I told him with tear in my eyes.

As I recalled from my aunt, "You should give your son to someone else to take care and to raise him," said the doctor.

"I cannot let my son go away from me," said my Mom.

However, my aunt hit me on my back to make me cry so the doctor felt sympathy for our situation and kept me with my Mom. "I have to hit you hard to make you cry," my aunt said. The doctor was also from before 1975 and had sympathy for the situation that my Dad was in the communist camp and only my Mom could take care of me. He tried his best to help my Mom quickly recover.

Each time I talk about this story; my eyes are all wet with tears. It is very emotional. My aunt also tries to help us to keep my Mom and me stay together. But she was so young. At that time, she was around 15 years or so.

"His Mom and him are so pitiful at this time," said my grandmother. My grandmother and my aunt's eyes are wet with tear each time we talk about this story. She also admires my Mom. If my Mom did not keep me with her, I do not know how my life will be different now. This thing shows how my Mom inspired me and did not let go of anything in her life. The Mom that I need and the Mom that led us and took care us. My Mom was left with four children after my Dad was in the communist camp. So my mother really self-disciplined and motivated herself. Without leaving her child starving and devastated. Our grandparents helped us by giving us rice and food from time to time. But my grandmother told my mother that, when she married my Dad, it is her own life; she had to accept it whether it is the tough life or easy life. But without my Mom's self motivation and discipline we would not be united and be here at I am today.

I learned that my Mom had a goal and discipline to lead her family and to take care of each of us in the family. She worked so hard day and night to raise us. Whenever I think about what happened, my eyes grow wet with tears and I really appreciate and admired my Mom.

My Mom, Dad, grandma, and aunt have had the greatest impact on me and inspired me. The lesson that I learned here is that, we need to have someone to inspire and to look up to. As a child, these people were around me and inspired me so much. My sister and brothers also inspired me well because we were all working hard. I only have one older sister. My sister is also very dedicated and works hard and is able to see things. She can do business and help my Mom.

For these years that my Dad was away from home, my Mom was able to step up and lead our family and raised us. The endless hours of loving, caring, and hard working from Mom provided food and raised us and kept us together. My Mom also was able to save gold to pay for my older brother to escape Vietnam by boat.

8

Change of Our Inner and Outer Peace

Every step in our mind and our thoughts lead us and affects our emotions and our behavior.

We have the ability to adapt to such situations when the environment around us changes. The change from outer influences, such as environment, (our thought, culture, weather, climate) life situation, family, etc. and the change inside us (point of view, prospective, and physical, mental behavior). They both interact and effect each other. The inner changes have an effect on our behavior and respond to the outer change. It has such an impact on the outcome and our acting and behavior. One we can control, the inner change; it can help us stay calm and lead us to handle things well.

The daily activity and our absorption of things from outside could impact our inner behavior. We learn more in our own experience as we grow about how to handle things and stay calm to solve problems. We tend to decide and make decisions based on our emotions. This is because the situation, or such external situations, impact our response.

In my situation, my decisions and responses are normally better once I stay calm and think things over. We learn, experience, and improve the way we respond and handle things. As young children, we tend to do the thing through our own emotions but as we grow older, we tend to think about the impact on others and pros and cons when handling things. This only happens through our own learning and through our own experiences, but the way we handle things could be improved by thinking them over and giving ourselves time. Do not make quick decisions when we are in hurry or in stress. Try to have good physical health and calm emotions when we have to deal with a difficult situation.

We need to stay healthy with great physical attributes and emotions. We all know that, in order to keep us in good health and great physically, we need to not only eat healthy but also need to do physical exercise to keep our mind in great health.

To keep our mental and inner peace healthy, we can meditate and focus to improve inner peace. The meditation each day, and yoga, could improve our inner peace. The meditation and focus on our self could improve our mentality and keep us in great mental happiness inside. Each second, each minute, and each hour of keeping our thoughts in great peace could keep and lead us to more happiness and to handling things in effectively and more efficiency.

Every step in our mind and our thought leads us and affects our emotions and our behavior. Once I know all the pros and cons, I can deeply think and follow my heart to think about all of possible situations, what the outcome might be, whatever its effects will be on me, my family. I also listen to and follow my heart to see what is the best outcome.

In 2010, after finishing my Ph.D., I could go to take a research scientist position to work in the industry and to follow up with and carried on with my dissertation work but it was about three-and-a-half hours away from home. But with another research position in the national laboratory in the US, I would work in a different area that is not much related to my dissertation work.

"Listen and follow your heart," Dr. Stan, a research scientist at Oregon State University, replied to me. I talked to him sometime to get advice because he is not in our department and would be able to see and talk about the things that are not related to school or personal issues. It took me a while and I was so worried about these choices and the decision I made. But as I review and analyze the entire possible outcome and pros and cons, advantage and disadvantage of both choices and listen to my heart for what I want, I was able to decide which position to take.

I feel blessed and valued the comment that Dr. Stan gave me. I learned that, even with just a word or comment, people can help a lot. I said goodbye to Dr. Stan when I left the school. Beside Dr. Stan, my formal advisor also helped me with completion of my doctoral work. I said good-bye to my advisor, Dr. Norman, after working with him for three years. He is one of the smartest professors I ever worked with. I so admire him for his guidance, his organizational skills, his leadership in everything, and in research.

9

Idaho Conference: A Story of Achievement and the Pathway We Have Chosen

Work hard for your goal and no matter how much it takes, follow your heart and your dream. You will be successful and be recognized.

Each of us values the things important in life: we desire to be recognized and to be known.

During the time doing my graduate work, we had chances to travel to different places for conferences and talks. One of the most memorial conferences that I never forgot was the one in Boise, Idaho It was a conference that was organized by Forest Products Society. We were able to submit both talk and poster presentations. I did both a talk and a poster. During the conference, there was some free time for us to explore Idaho. We went outside the city and kept exploring things around. We do not have any plans for where to go and what to bring. None of us brought any water. We kept walking away from the hotel that we stayed and explored thing around Boise. After just walking away from the city for an-hour-and-a-half, we reached the bottom of the mountain. There are mountains located around Boise. The city was covered with mountains and at the lower latitude. We then reached the bottom of the mountain, but on the top of that mountain there was a really big cross. At the bottom of the mountain, we already saw the view of the city but not very clearly. We saw the trail that we can walk up there to reach that cross. we had no water and I was really thirsty, but we all walked along and cannot go back, after another two hours of walking and climbing, we reached the middle of the mountain. I was really tired and thirsty because I did not drink before I left the hotel, and now it was almost four hours after we left the hotel. We were just one by one walking up to the mountain. I was at the end of the line. I felt really tired but with my desire I kept walking and following my colleagues. But I already viewed almost everything about the city when I looked back at the city.

"Keep going, Edward," Kai encouraged me.

"Okay, I am trying," I replied.

After almost an hour, I was so thirsty, my head was dizzy and we were all almost falling. It was because of over four hours not drinking and continuous walking I was dehydrated. I felt really tired and was almost falling.

"Walk up here and look, Edward," Kai yelled.

I saw the view of the city. It was beautiful. I could see each and every building of the city; it was so incredible.

"Are you glad that you made it up here, Edward?" Kai asked me.

"Wow, yes. It is so beautiful. I am so glad I made it," I replied.

We were also able to view roughly the location of our hotel. We also saw people that carved their name in the wood underneath the cross. The cross is so big and stands up magnificently. Standing there, I forgot about and was relieved of much of my thirst and my dizziness subsided, and I felt the magnificence of the view. How large the cross is and how beautiful the city. The nature that my eye observed and my head was thinking about the word ACHIEVEMENT and forgot all of my suffering and how hard was everything I had been through in order to reach the top of the mountain.

***

On the day I graduated, I still remember the feeling from when we passed and walked in the middle where all the undergraduates needed to yield for us. We walked in the middle. The students are lined up and we walked passed them in the middle. This special ceremony is only for people who have earned doctoral degrees. I felt so happy and so respected by others. I also felt the reward of so many years of hard work and I now had the reward. The reward of recognition and respect from our peers and from people who earned bachelors and masters degrees.

The graduation ceremony program printed out our names, our previous bachelors, and master degrees, and our dissertation work.

Graduate school

"I have to retake the qualifying exam," said my college friend as OSU. We felt very terrified to find out that our hopes and dreams of thing that we can do and will accomplish could not become reality. I really saw the terror and tears in my college friend's eyes. The Ph.D. qualification is the hardest and most challenging examination for each of us. But we have to go through this stage in order to become Ph.D. candidates and complete our requirements. In order to complete the Ph.D. exam we needed to get accepted to the program, complete all course requirements, pass the preliminary exam, and qualify example and then the final exam. The preliminary exam normally compiles exams questions, of course, and materials that we need to master, and could be both written and an oral presentation. Then there is the quality exam. The quality exam comprised written and oral presentations. The written part of the quality exam could be compiled of exam questions or developing a proposal and an oral presentation. After the quality exam then we can become Ph.D. candidates and work on our research and finish our final with a written dissertation and defend our dissertation work with the presentation. The complete process could vary in length and time depending on a person to person but typical it is three to five years after finishing a master degree.

I was told that graduate school is one of the best times in our life. And yes, it is true, but for most of us, we need to complete our requirement to graduate. But there are students that do not finish and complete their requirement and do no graduate.

"I have to retake the qualifying exam," said George my friend. I really felt sad for him and worried about me as well. But with time and discipline I prepared well and passed my exam. We really suffered and worried about the exam because we cannot complete the requirements and we cannot graduate if we do not meet the requirements. But each process guides us and helps us move up and prepared us to be a better researcher, scientist, or educator.

My professor tried to motivate us by telling us that we need to focus and have a positive attitude in what we are doing. Love what you do. And yes, it is true. I realized that we needed to love what we do and find the enjoyable part for each of our own work. Sure the process of completing graduate school is not easy; it involved hard work, dedication, and independence and much effort to make it through. But we earned the respect and recognition.

10

My Dad's Story

We tend to view and see different things when our living environment and our life change or we lose things that we love. We then started to realize and value the lost more and adjust ourselves. These adjustments and changes made us improve our way of thinking, things around us, and become more responsible for these living changes.

My Dad was in the communist prison camp for seven years, and after release, he still had to report and be overseen for another seven years. He worked during the day and tried hard to do service in the camp. There were several times, he told us, that he was almost killed but on the way an office trying to force him to walk away from the camp to shoot him but saw his prisoner friend and called his name so the officer released him. The officer tried to punish him without other people knowing because my Dad did not please him so he got mad and wanted to kill him. The human life in this situation did not weigh much. It's the weight of nothing. So because one of his friends saw, the officer was afraid of others knowing so he released him. He was so scared and said that his life was saved by his friend. He had been through a lot of suffering and trying to serve in the prison camp so he could reunite with us.

After Saigon fell, he talked to my Mom and my grandmother, saying that he needed to report to the Vietnam government, and was told roughly that he would be there for seven days but it turned out that he was there for seven years.

After he was released, he still lived their in his nightmares. We really saw the difference and how his personality changed. He became scared of everything, even the police walking by on the street. He always got scared. He cannot even convince himself that he did not do anything wrong. In the camp, he had to serve and obey without reason, without knowing if it made sense or not. I remember a lot of times back there, any paperwork and anything that we need to go and talk to the police about, my Mom is the person who would do the talking and negotiate with them. I did not talk about the upper-level people. I just talked about the people in the small town who just want to control and think that they can do whatever they can to control us.

***

"When my Dad was 33 years old, he was in the communist prison camp and lost all of his money, the house was bombed and destroyed, so he lost everything," said my older sister. This made me relieved because I had lost money and the family was falling apart. Back in 1975, my Dad lost all the money he had gained, lost his house, and was placed in the communist camp. He left behind my Mom that was pregnant with me, with two older brothers, and one sister. His life was turning in a different direction. Although, I was little, I still loved him and heard a lot of the great stories about what happened in the camp and the way he tried to survive himself. But he also has lots of friend that he met there and they later become lifetime friends and even when they went to the US, they were still connected and keep in touch with each other. I still was not able to feel the emotions of my Dad until recently with the things I lost in my life, my family, work, and money. For a while, I lost my feeling, my emotion, my trust, and my motivation to do the anything in life. However, after thinking about these words that my sister told about my Dad, I realized that it is the only stage that I need to go through. I started to appreciate my Dad more about things that he has been through, about his personality, the way he acted toward us, his temper, and things.

I feel blessed to have him as my Dad. He has been with me throughout my life. We have had such wonderful times together, even though my Dad has suffered and this has had some effect on him from during the war and in the camp. He was in a car accident and his head suffered more than 10 stitches and the crack in his head was about 2 to 3 inches long. Dad was told that he may not make it, but he made it but was in a coma for several days. This incident and the effect of the camp really effected his personality. He is very easy to get upset when things do not go his way.

During the time in the camp, he made a lot of stuff for us, such as necklaces for my sister to wear and also hand carry bag by bamboo for me. He used whatever materials he could find in the camp to make these to give to us. These emotions and the feeling of caring for his family and doing whatever he could for his family that he could made me admire him.

11

Economic Great Recession 2007-2009

"The poor long for riches, the rich long for heaven, but the wise desire tranquility!" Source: Unknown

It is great to see and always be aware of things happening around us. That can help us prevent bad things from happening to us and improve our living and survival chances in life and in any situation.

Sometimes we follow our own path, our road, and do not look back or have time to view the things happening around us. We all think that what we are doing is right. Sometimes in business and life, and even in relationships, we need to listen to other perspectives and advice from people who have more experience, who have been through tough times in life.

We need to know when to stop. In doing business and such things involving money, we need to manage and be constantly aware of things around us and what is happening. We need to do a great deal of interacting with economic and recognize when and how to make a good move. We can miss the opportunities for improving our life and our success. Once the opportunities are passed, we may not able to go back to the same stage. These opportunities could lead us in a totally different direction. We can create much joyful, loss or suffering. One of the biggest events in my life is about economic crisis of the Great Recession of 2007. The 2007-2009 US economic Great Recession had much effect on my investments and real estate properties. The investment depreciated and I lost a big chunk of investments and properties. I was not able to go back to the same stage as I was before. But looking back, I could have improved and handled things better. "So how do I do better?" I constantly ask myself. In the same time of the Great Recession, I also lost my job. I had been working there for over two years and I really enjoyed. I did not have enough money to pay for my mortgages and I could not sell some of my properties because they had so much depreciation in value. I really learned a great lesson after going through this economic crisis. I tried hard and managed well to lead me out of this economic crisis to reduce expensive overhead costs and used up all my savings. After I went through this crisis, I realized that a lot of people lost money, but there was such a large amount of people who benefited in this crisis. I saw several people in my family and relatives who would able to buy their properties with cheaper prices than before. I also learned that we also need a backup plan for everything we do in our life, especially in business.

Sometimes we stick to our own design and our own mess for a while. I did not have a chance to change and move on quickly. Because these losses are so great it takes more time to recovery.

"I told you to sell these properties and take all the gain," my Mom said. However, the situation is so different than what people see. These properties are my for-rent properties and they barely make enough money to pay for the mortgage. Some of the older properties that I bought longer ago, I make positive cash flow with these.

We stick to our own design and our own problems. We do not have a chance to stop and realize it. We did not have another perspective or point of view. We did not have other options. Sometimes we do not have another great option. Then we just have to keep continuing our own path even though we know in the current situation it is not great, but from time to time it is much better and we learn much from great experiences by continuing with it even if we fail. I know that in life, everyone fails here and there but I challenge myself because, in business, it can be failure that we can learn a great deal from it. I also learned a lesson of standing up from there when I fall. I did not learn that before. If in case the business plans are not a success, then what is the percent of success? We need to think about that, and as we go through the situation and experience more, we learn more and more, and we are able to realize how we can do it better when the situation happens again or we have experience to deal with problems that arise in our daily life. We start analyzing it and seek things for improving and the ability to appreciate and learn our own lesson from our own mistake.

As I go through my life experience and keep in my mind that no one is perfect; we all can make mistakes in every aspect of our life but we need to learn how to stand back up again. We can learn a lesson from our mistakes. Once we realize and learn the lesson in life, it changes the way we think and our perspective in our own thought. We then think of more positive activities, and become certain that we can go through all situations ad problems in our life.

12

Never Ask What's Wrong, Why or Criticize the System

When you are clutching something in your hands without letting go, then all you have is that. If you let it go, then you have the opportunity to choose other things. If a person is always looking at thing from the same prospective and do not let go of things, then their knowledge, their personal growth, and wisdom can only reach that level.

Learn how to accept things, even if sometimes it does not make sense at the moment, but you will find out it makes sense later. That is a lesson I learned when working in research and even teaching. Every one of us knows that, our knowledge and the ability to absorb, to understand the things around us, are limited. That is why we need to accept the things, even if they do not make sense at that moment. Some of the things do not even make sense now, but it can come to us again and at the right time and right moment, we will be able to understand, to feel it, to appreciate it. It takes some time in the learning process to accept things in our mind. This could be demonstrated when we are working on experiments doing chemical reaction.

Every one of us should took general or organic chemistry courses in the past or will take it some day; we need to follow directions step by step to make a successful experiment. That is the processes and procedure that we must follow to complete the specific experiment.

"You need to follow the exact steps and processes that you wrote on your pre-lab questions," I said to the student. During the time at the University of Washington, I had to teach two chemistry lab sections each Tuesday and Thursday. I need to prepare the exact amount of chemicals, the exact weight percent of solution silver nitrate in the exact amount of acid sulfuric to get the crystal precipitate. It also needs to heat for the exact time and temperature.

"If it does not work, try to move on with different ideas or with different things if the thing does not work out for you now," said Dr. Yadama, a professor at UW. I learned that, sometimes in doing research or work, do not ask or critique the system, it only causes us more time and wastes our time and brings negative thoughts. This prevents us from moving up and also creates negative thoughts, and a negative work environment.

Taiwan is a great example to see how much paperwork needs to be done even just for an order to buy simple materials. We need to get approval with the lists of items, the quote and approval from so many offices. There, it is about 10 different stamps in several offices and buildings and layers that we need to go through even before the order is processed. There are so many unnecessary stamps and processes. This is such a waste of time and effort.

"This will not work in the U.S.," said Dr. Chang.

"But if we do not follow these steps, we will not get the order done here," I said. *The system is the system. We cannot attempt to change the system. Because it is the way it is. If we cannot change it, then we just need to admit it and move on, even though we know that it just creates so many unnecessary steps and processes.*

13

Effect of My Family and How I View Myself

No matter how tough or how hard your life is, with time, you can heal and move on.

Throughout my life, I learned that people who are disabled or who are not normal usually have some special skill or talented. For people who are not normal, their life is not busy with the daily activities or they do not spend so much time on normal activities such as daily outlook or spend much time with friends or not used their time efficiently. *I found this, these people normally spend their time and focus more on some skill and this helps them to develop these particular skills into something special and they become talented. We see that there are so many abnormal people who have so many special skills and talents around us. This is not because they were all born with it, but that they only pay attention to developing some special skill or spend their effort and energy in dreaming to develop these special skills. This is because their mind and perspective is focused more on these special skill and they end up with more time and practice as their live goes on.* This also helps to show that these people have so much discipline and motivation and help themselves overcome these disadvantages and develop new special skills and talent. They are people who did not see their disadvantage and disability as many disadvantages in their own respect but also normally see this disadvantage is just part of their life and just as normal.

As a little kid, I did not see my disadvantages in my family as things that prevent me from growing up and preventing me from attending and doing well in school. I overcome my difficulties by focusing on the problem, focusing on school, working hard, and motivating myself to deal with this difficulty. When I got older, I also saw the story of my Dad and my Mom to motivate myself and overcome my suffering and my stress.

"At the age of 33 years old, my Dad was in the communist camp and stayed there for seven years. He lost his house and lost almost everything. He left behind a pregnant wife with a house that was destroyed because of the Viet Nam war without money," said my sister Huong. These words came up again and again in my mind.

The story of when my Dad went to the camp and how hard everything was that he went through motivates me and helps me to find and have energy to overcome and continue on my chosen path.

Learn that no mater how hard life is or what you went through and suffered, with time you can heal. We could always view or compare with others that went through greater suffering to relief stress, so it could improve and make ourselves feel relieved or feel less stressful and help us to motive ourselves.

My parents went through so much suffering and much loss because of the war but with focus, love, discipline, and always believing that we will be united, helped them get through this suffering and tragedy.

Things happen for a reason. I was away from family and sometimes I even lost track of how my daughter was doing, even when she was sick or how she was doing in school.

Therefore, we need to set priorities and value the most important thing in life and do it as quickly as possible. Make a to-do list and follow it each day. Look at and improve your daily notes and activities and follow them well. That is what I learned in order to be on the top of thing and to gain happiness and to relieve stress.

14

Interactions and Role Models Who Have Inspired My Dreams

Role models have an impact on much of my actions and my response and my desire for higher education.

Be happy and fulfilled; be happy and responsible for whatever you do, be positive and try to connect with the daily work and do hard work. Throughout my experiences, I learned from hard work how to do things and study. We went through each and every step and it is very hard to go through and hard to accomplish. So we need to value ourselves and reward ourselves and see a positive impact.

All things are possible, so our mind can generate possible results to make a positive impact on others.

So experience the emotions and suffering, which are good and bad throughout our live so we can make a positive impact on ourselves. We will become more productive and do great work.

When I was young, everyone asked me, what I want to become "An engineer," I replied. I do not even know what type of engineer I wanted to be. Back when I was little in Vietnam, we were not exposed much to the world. My knowledge about the world, in general, was very limited. Not until I grew up and went to the US, I realize there are so my type of engineers. Engineer is the basic term referring to one who obtains the bachelor degree and focuses on the engineering aspect or focuses more on the application of it.

When I moved further to my graduate school and research world, I also learned the word "science." Science is referring more to the depth of the scientific explanation of such a problem. More focus on the science, the principle, and the explanation of things around us in terms of science and the law of matter. The law of matter refers to the first principle, which is F=MA or the internal force of materials (F) or matter is equal to its mass (M) and its acceleration (A). The interaction force between two things is the combination of attractive and repulsive force.

Therefore, in nature, the attractive force and repulsive force can be the combination and the resultant force is the next force and is the combination of the two. The same thing happens in our daily life, such as personal relationships or the interaction between humans. It is the same explanation of the combination of forces of the next attractive and repulsive forces between each individual member of us.

15

Looking Back

When looking back at my story and my journey that I went through, surely it is a tough life with lots of change but I really appreciate and am thankful for it. It is so great that I have been through this and experienced it. I can feel it and have a great sense of it. I have been through great times and bad times. Through these experiences, it helped me define myself and define who I am. It is a valuable lesson that I have learned in life. We need to focus on our goal and our desire of doing great things for ourselves and people around us. Making positive impacts to the planet that we live in. I feel very fortunate and blessed. Because there is so much devastation and so many people do not have a chance and opportunity to do things like I do, or be exposed to things like I am. I feel that I owe it to myself and this is the reason why I wrote this book. I am hoping that people can learn from the experiences that I have and make a positive impact in life and people around us. Because each second, each minute, and each hour that we are living on this planet is a gift from God, so I make sure I use it greatly and make a positive impact on people around us.

***

As a student, choosing the major and thing that you like to do is very important because it represents you and reshapes your image from others and helps you view and see your own greatness and your limitations. Education and school only help us with the ability to write, read, and communicate with people. But most important is the desire to do the things and focus on what we want to do. So we not only set the priority on things we want to do but also our purpose and things that we can do, the positive things in life. The results are the outcome of the process. The results are the outcome of the work, but sometimes we need to do and when we are evolving in this, we learn these processes. And during these processes we can learn, and new ideas are come along. This is always true and happening when I do research, work, and do the things in life. I always find a new thing and new discovery. The end results are sometimes not important. But when we do it, we went through the process. And do not feel the regret we would feel if we did not do it. And we do not give out self-question with regret such that, "If I did not do that, what thing would happen here? And If I do something different and pick this choice or that choice, will my life will be different? Would I be on a different path?"

A lot of time, I do things and follow them, but I feel that it is not much benefit, but more about enjoying finishing it. The only thing is that, we try our best, no matter what the outcome is. Through the process, we learn it and observe, and know what can we learn from this experience and what is the lesson of it, so we can improve and do it better and learn from there. Therefore, our mind constantly thinks that unless we are experienced, we have observed, we saw, we then appreciated and developed our knowledge and this takes us to the next level.

Every one of us always makes mistakes in life but as we realize and admitted it, we can learn so much from our mistakes to improve ourselves. Through these mistakes, it helps me to listen and think things over to improve myself. We contently went through this learning process in life. But we need to review ourselves and ask what we have done, what we have accomplished in each stage of our life. Doing this helps us stay focused and motivate ourselves.

I did not think and did not have very clear vision on things in life that I wanted or wished to accomplish but once I got older and beyond my thirties, I started to ask lots of questions about me, myself, and what I have accomplished and want to do next.

What Have I Accomplished?

At each stage of my life, I think and rethink, asking myself what I have done, and accomplished thus far in my life and what do I want to be next. The only way is to write down a list and stay focused on it each day. After I arrived in the U.S., I heard my cousin talking about University of Washington (UW) and how good it is, and then I really said to myself that I needed to attend it and finish my bachelor degrees there. This wishing became my dream. I then built my own dream catcher for wishing to finish my bachelors degree at UW and hung it next to my bed, so each day I can see it and it keeps reminding me about this and how and what I need to do in order to accomplish this. This is the process I went through for all of my work and throughout my education. This process helps me to define my goal, my purpose, my reason, and what do I need to do to accomplish it.

Through education, one needs to have a great place to study, chance to learn new things, and your goal and desire to accomplish it. What will take you from where you are now to the level you want to be? Is your environment and the things around you able to allow you to get to the level you want to be at or do you need to change the environment, or do you need to improve yourself in order to accomplished that? This process helps me to improve my own thought and my own study. Like how much time I need to spend for each of my courses, what materials I need to complete, when and how to do it. During the process of learning and obtaining this, I can be able to accomplish my goal and fulfill my desire.

Be a Servant and Serve Others

I learned that being a servant and doing service for others is a great way of improving and accomplishing goals. In school, a lot of time I had been able to help people around me to study. Each exam, I was able to study and master the material prior and much before the exam came. We usually reviewed and went over material before the exam day.

"We should go over and review the materials again to help our exam," talking to Van I said.

"Sure we can go to the Engineering library to review at 3:00 pm today," Van replied. We met and I reviewed the materials and went over it with Van and another classmate.

There was a problem in thermodynamics that we needed to know and I was sure it would be on the exam. Talking to other classmates, I said I was able to help others to review the materials. Through the processing of teaching others, it forces me to learn and even master the materials. You can master the materials once you are able to teach, because teaching to others, even to your classmates, will force you to be a master on that topic and your brain is constantly thinking of and finding ways to master the materials and this area.

Be a servant to others and love things that you do. You have the passion and design to fulfill it. It is help to motivate ourselves in school and in work and every aspect of our life. We cannot change others' thinking, but we can change ours and help to improve things.

My former boss has a very bad temper. Every deadline on turning in proposals or meeting the deadline, he has a temper and easily gets upset if things are not going well. This prevents us from easily expressing our ideas, creates a stressful work environment and sometimes makes me very scared. One time he hit the table and even kicked the chair. One time I tried to talk to him but made him get even more upset about it. So, after a couple of attempts to talk to him, I know how he could react. So every time a similar incident occurred, I just think of away to get away out of the situation to make him calm and get myself to stop thinking and stop talking about it or move to a different subject, just be quiet and do not talk about it or make myself accept the situation and do not want to judge or confront him. When he calmed down, he always came and apologized for what happened or for the bad word or the way he got mad. There are several times that he apologized and said sorry for what happened. I realized that sometimes people have temper issues then instead of changing them, I just accepted it and do not want to change them. Instead I just find a way to improve things and do better on my part and adjust myself to improve the situation. This always ends up with better results.

Do not want to change or attempt to change others, instead change yourself.

Discussion With Others

As long we listen and give people enough time they will always surprise us with how much they know and how much they can do.

"You should do this and do that, etc." our family member or friends always said. We should take advice and listen to others and learn from others because it is greatly advised with the different perspective. The person gives great advice who has already have been through the tough situation and have learned the lessons. Because we all come to the US at the same time and my parents do not have any experience of thing in the US. We tend to almost ignore the advice of them about the US in general. *This is one of the mistakes I make and also see lots of young people make. I learned much later in life that our parents are normally right on general things and their perspective in life and their experiences that they went through, including tragedy during and after the war and economic difficulty.*

***

People we meet and come in our life: whether meeting new students or friends, all left us with a footprint and a valuable lesson as long we listen to it. I really appreciate and feel fortunate once I meet people and learn their experience and things that they accomplished in life. What is their point of view and how do they survive and grow? I learned that, as long as I listen and give them enough time, they always surprise me with how much they know and how much they can do. One day I have an appointment with Apple Care to diagnose my Mac hardware and meet John. Back there, I was really interested and did some research on my own about zero energy houses, renewable energy, and wind power.

"Hello," I said.

"Hello," the guy said.

"What is your name?" I asked.

"My name is John," he replied.

"What brought you here today?" I asked.

"I need to diagnose my Mac desktop," John replied. The discussion went on and on about the computer and then started onto the renewable energy and wind energy. I just did not believe how much he knew about it and he even has the wind power to generate electric for his house. He later gave me his home address and invited me to visit his house to see his wind power that he build by himself.

Prospective From Other Cultures

In order to understand others, we need to learn and understand ourselves first.

I had a chance to travel to different places and to different countries to see different things and meet different people. I had a chance to learn new languages, new cultures, and a chance to stay in, work and see the new environment. I feel really joyful once I open my heart and accept the differences. These also reflect me and force me to find out more and review our culture.

I was so grateful to the new environment, new friends that I was exposed to, where I can learn and be exposed to another environment and see the different cultures and different things.

We can review and compare other cultures and see the good things and bad things about our own respect. These advantages and disadvantages that we learned and picked up from our own and new cultures helped and served us well when talking to or communicating with people. It is very valuable and very important to reflect our culture with other cultures. This will reflect about ourselves, our own image. I also learn that, in order to understand about others, we need to learn and understand our own culture first.

In the US, the wife will be less likely to stay home or give up her job and career to take care of a baby or become a housewife and do things around the house but in Vietnam and Asian the wife can give up her career and stay home to take care of the baby and do house work in the house. In Vietnam, the wife can step back and stay behind the husband to take care and for the good of the family.

The Beauty in Every Culture and the Memorization of Student Life

We all missed our childhood and student life that we have been through. Royal Poinciana witnessed and shared many ups and down, joys and sorrows, of the yearly exam in our learning for our time in school.

Talking about "student life" is not completed if we do not talk about Royal Poinciana or "Hoa Phượng" and a long dress "Áo dài" or long white dress of the student with the Vietnam traditional hat "Nón lá". What a lot of memories and thrills.

Traditional Vietnamese long dress with hat and Royal Poincian

Traditional Vietnamese long dress with Royal Poincian and bicycle

Traditional Vietnamese long dress with hat at Binh Quoi

Traditional Vietnamese long dress with hat standing
next to coconut tree at Van Thanh, Sai-Gon

"Here I can help," said a pedestrian, while I was taking pictures of Royal Poinciana or "Hoa Phượng or " in Vietnam. This flower has a special meaning for students because the flowers bloom at the end of the school year and it is the time that we have to be away from friends and classmates.

Phượng vĩ witnessed and shared many ups and down, joys and sorrows, of the yearly exam in our learning for the time in school. In Vietnam, it is represented and reminds us of a time in school and the time that we have to be away from friends and classmates.

There is so many memories that I remember when talking about school and "student life" or "Tuổi Học Trò" in Vietnam. It is the Hoa Phượng and Áo dài.

Students in VietNam are normally required to wear traditional long dress "Áo dài" for school. The long dress showed the beauty and the shyness of the schoolgirl. It expresses the beauty and pureness of the girls. Basically, the long dress expresses the beauty and all the pureness and beauty of the females in general. The long dress also connects to the Royal Poinciana flower, because it expresses the student's life and many stories about the student life. These memories, happiness, joy, and also sometimes sad stories and love stories during the learning in student life all express the beauty of the long dress and Royal Poinciana flower. However, in the U.S. students are might not required to wear a uniform in public school.

Foods

I went through a lot of emotions and sad stories, but it made me stronger and more experienced and I see things that I never saw, traveling to different places and seeing the different cultures.

We are able to cook many traditional Vietnamese foods in the US but we also eat other regular foods such as burgers, sandwiches, and hotdogs. Traditionally, most Asians eat a lot of rice. We normally eat rice almost everyday. The first year, I really ate a lot of rice and started to eat less and less rice at I grew older but started to pick up different foods, such as sushi and other Italian foods and Mexican foods. I not only eat our own traditional noodle foods, but now balance this with other foods as well.

16

Grand Cayman Island Experience in Life and Scuba Diving or Snorkeling

When exposed to a different culture, we have more chance to improve, exchange and reflect on our own.

I went through school and failed and keep failing but I still completed and finished my degrees. I went to St. Mathew Medical School in Grand Cayman Island near Florida with the hope of obtaining my Medical Doctor degree so I can do medical research but had a problem with memorization, and it was too expensive for the cost of living and tuition. I was not able to support myself and cannot fit well in the environment.

In medical school, professors also did not treat us as well as at our graduate school. As graduate school, as I did with my masters before I went to medical school, I can teach and support myself. But at medical school, I met lots of the great friends that had much impact on my life. I have met a lot of local people and lifetime friends there. At Grand Cayman Island, the police there do not wear a gun. The island is so surrounded with peace and joy. The day starts with running in the morning for about a mile and breakfast and then I went to school. Compared to my first school, this school as even more different types of people, people from Europe, from Canada and so on, but the majority are from the US. I was exposed to another culture there; their lifestyle is very different than Vietnamese but very similar to the US but they are very friendly people. The island is surrounded with people, mainly tourists and there so many cruise ships stopped by there during the summer time. This also is the first time in my life that I know and experience from watching the show about pirates. The show starts with pirate who are kidnapping and taking away treasures of people and boats and whoever passed by there.

"Are you going to the scuba diving course with me Hy?" I asked.

"I don't think I can swim that far. I'm just gonna go snorkeling, " Hy replied.

It turns out that is true. After a couple of days of studying about scuba diving in general, about the sea and how to avoid dangerous waves and so on, we went to the nice beach with very deep water levels that was used for scuba diving. On the first day in the water class, we needed to first pass the test by swimming to the small boat that was parked on the beach and swim back and stand swinging for a while in the water. It was really hard to do that if you did not do very well and did not have enough practice. Several people could not make it in the first round where they are drowning and vomiting. We then train on how to breath and how the water gets into our nose and we are still breathing. It is very uncomfortable at first and it takes practice. There were several times I felt I was drowning and could not make it where my head was dizzy and I drank a large volume of water. Several times I thought I could not make it, but I was able to mange and went through. I was so happy and felt that I could achieve something in my life.

I realize that it is same in our life. We can enjoy the beauty of the underwater and the sea, even without knowing how to scuba dive like my friend who chose just snorkeling. But if I did not do it and pass my course for scuba diving, I would not be able to go through these experiences and finally enjoy the beauty of the underwater and experience of the achievement and completion. It is the same at the pathway or turns that we make in life. We will not experience it and will not observe and be able to come at the top or next level if we choose not to do it. Even if we suffer and went through a tough time, we can still reach the final goal of joy and happiness. The happiness of seeing and viewing the underwater, the person who knows how to scuba dive can view both the surface of the water and deep underwater level and snorkeling only causes us to be able to view the surface of the water but still enjoy and be happy about it. This is just another prospective in life, but the one who did snorkeling only limited his or herself to only one view.

****

"The apple doesn't fall far from the tree." Vietnamese folk poem

I did not realize time went by so fast and we were already in the US for so many years now. We did not realize that we were able to adapt to a new culture and new environment so quickly. We tried and adjusted ourselves so we could survive in the new environment, new country. We do not use clothes that we brought along from our country that were not appropriate and not convenient to wash and dry. Before we left VietNam, our grandmother kept reminding us not bring things that are not suitable or difficult to wash and dry. We brought several traditional hats and artificial flowers for New Year, ochna itegerrima and marumi kumquat that we can give to our aunt and uncles.

We have been changing our outfits and things to help us adapt to the environment like the outfit that we bough when we arrived. The clothes that we brought from VietNam did not work so well for washing machines and driers so we had to buy new clothes. However, we still define and know our own roof, and still keep our traditional activities whenever we can. We normally gather and the older usually give money to the younger after the younger tell a good word, wishing the olders well during the Luna New Year. Traditionally, we believe that the first day of a new year has an effect on the entire year so we prepared and normally wore nice or new clothes for the first day of the year if it was possible. We tend to eat a great meal during the New Year and we can prosper and do well for the whole year. Each end of the Luna calendar year, we also review and see what we have been doing and what we will want to do for next year. Our mother normally asks what we have been doing from each of us and sees what we can do for our next year.

Traditional Luna New Year "Tet" in VietNam

We were tried hard to adapt to a new environment. We were changed or adjusted ourselves to fit into it in a good way. But still keep our original roof. We still have to keep the traditional such as making "sweet rice cake" during New Year and making rice noodle "or Phở in Vietnamese" whenever we can. We normally made these traditional Vietnamese foods and eat it at least one to two times per month.

I also learned that trying to wear appropriate clothes, follow directions, do not run away from police, do not stay out or walk by ourselves when the sun goes down., etc.

*** Balance of the Two Cultures ***

Two different cultures (Vietnamese and USA), we have two different lifestyles, therefore I need to balance out these cultures' differences. These two cultures also have two different ideas about how to live our life and how to observe and respond to things in nature. In the US, normally, whatever thing happened, we need to call the police and try to help out the people first. For example, people in a coma or who stop breathing. Unlike in Vietnam, whenever something happened, we first try to help them to survive by whoever knows how to do CPR can help the person who stops breathing. The police will not come in. The response to an emergency is much slower and different in Vietnam compared to the US.

Traditional Lunar New Year "Tet" gathering in Seattle Center, WA, USA

The traditional celebration is also different, comparing in the US to Vietnam. We still participate in celebrating New Year and also recreating traditional Luna New Year by decorating the house with ochna itegerrima and marumi kumquat "hoa mai or hoa đào", make sweet rice cake, and even give money to the younger people. This tradition still goes on and is passed on from our parent to us in the US. We cannot bring everything from Vietnam to the US so we only can do these celebrations to gather family together. We then end up with, besides the regular holidays in the US, like Independence Day (July 4) Presidents Day, Memorial Day, Christmas holiday, Labor Day, and so on, we also have Luna New Year.

Besides the holiday, my Mom also tried to grow things such as vegetable and things that make it similar to vegetable in Vietnam as possible. So the culture is balanced and united in ourselves, so it in not the same and only one culture but the mix of the two. As long as they find a good fit and their desire what they want, everyone always find a good fit for them.

Everyone always found a good fit for them. We don't want a bad thing to happen to everyone of us. We need to adapt but also find a good fit for ourselves. Everyone has our own purpose, want something, and want to be recognized and a desire in life, but we need to define and continuously remind ourselves what is the true meaning and how do we want to accomplish it, how to fulfill out purpose.

***As long as everyone has benefit, they are
willing to contribute to the table***

We need to clearly know what our responsibilities are, be able to be of part a team. As long as everyone knows their's role and the importance of it. We are willing to contribute, volunteer, help, and contribute even more. We can contribute and create fun and so much energy in the environment that we are working on or in the environment that are part of. We are part of our bigger universe and part of our team. If we talk about our goal, purpose, and understand our common goal, our needs and designs everyone is willing to share and contribute and be responsible. One of these everyone achieves, there is so much energy in every action we make.

If we just think of too many negative things, then we will hurt ourselves. We will constantly think bad things will happen. Then it will affect us even more. Once the bad things happen, for example, "I did not handle things well" or "I did not handle thing so well," then I'm thinking of what I did wrong, and also thinking of both consequence, which also offers good things, not just negative aspects of it. Then things start to pick up or situate in such a way that I never experience. Because each of us does not know what things will happen next but as long we have possibilities and the goal we can serve and improve and do things better. Every one of us makes mistakes here or there in life and learns from the mistake.

When we keep ourselves in a positive mind-set, we can create momentum and energy to do the things and solve problems in a good manner and more efficiently. The possible aspect of our mindset creates more possibility and opportunities. Help and motivate and create momentum for us to do work more efficiently and effectively. Because the thing happened, then we realize it changed us and life will start to recovery.

Experiencing such a bad thing in life such as getting laid off, my family falling apart, loosing money in real estate made me realize that things are happening for a purpose for us to move into the next stage because it is still not totally in good shape and a peaceful life because I still did not enjoy it and did not fulfill my desire or our desire. I still felt I was missing something. We still are not able to live a peaceful life. As I start to look at things and analyze things in a possible direction. For a while, I feel so down and feel that life is not fair and even try to fix up things, change myself, and try to work things out but it still did not turn out the way I wanted. But when I start to accept whatever thing happened, I started to realize that it is not, it is just part of my actions on my insides and I have the responsibility to control of it. This helps me through my experience and my inner peace starts to heal. I do not thing much of negative things and my inner peace starts to change.

Thank you to people who did the good and bad things for me and thanks for every action that they respond to so I can learn and improve my strength and have such experience. Though difficulty and suffering and stress, I realized what I could do to improve myself and my situation.

***

Every part of the relationship such as between coworker, boss to employer, advisor to students, and even husband and wife, there is the interaction between the two. If there is no desire of both sides, then there is no common goal. Once there is no common goal between each member, then the relationship will not last long. I have the true-life experience in relationships with coworkers.

If there is less interaction, less care, but both sides still have things in common and one side still works for the common good, then it may help improve the relationship and still keep the relationship but (it will not serve the purpose) it may not satisfy both sides.

Why are there so many people that quit their job? I think this may not be mainly because of the workload but mainly the work environment. It is mainly people with bad relationships between supervisors and people on the team, between supervisors and people underneath them. If the boss knows how to lead the team and motive them well, he/she can create an effective environment and a fun place to work. Then it will improve the work environment, create a positive and more efficiently place to work, and motivate people. This is the same case as in the family once every individual family has participated and served the command and responsible, it can create a family place of full of joy and a place where each member in the house cares for and loves each other.

Every one of us has our own path and our own destination; one could have a very easy path and one could have very rough, difficulty path, so chose your path so your final destination can be reached. So our final goal and our final destination could be reached sooner.

So choose your path well. For students, we need to choose our major (our path) well so we can do well. The major can affect your path many years down the road. We can ask people around us and those who have experience to help us figure out the correct major that fits us so we can do it well and complete our education sooner. Different majors will lead to a different path. With the right path in the right time, and in the right moment, one can create and do a great thing and fulfill our destiny.

Every one of us needs some kind of help and has our own problems. But sometimes in life we have some great times and some bad or tough times, and whether we enjoy our path or not, we still need to go through it. The road we are walking on in life is never straight and never flat, so there are ups, downs and curves, but we need to focus and continue down our road.

We should create a more fun and more effective life and create a higher quality life, live our life such that it is enjoyable, living with purpose and a quality of life. When we are born, we cry and when we are dead, everyone else is crying but we are happy we served our purpose and fulfilled our goal. God gave us a responsibility for us to carry so we need to fulfill our destiny and by the end of our lifetime we can be happy to tell that we were happy to live our life and do not regret anything.

We are all the product and consequence of God's creation with being an effect on our own environment and the dynamics of changing in life. Life is an adventure, but we are being affected by our environment. We prefer our own comfort zone, but when we are not in our comfort zone, we also can learn and view different perspectives, different ideas, and challenges. Which will help us be better and become a better person.

Doing a dual Ph.D. with additional majors in graduate school is a challenge and I needed to be within my comfort zone and my specialization. I remember Dr. Johnson expressed an understanding of my knowledge and my ability to work in a different area, an area that I am not familiar with. I was worried and really having a hard time to fulfill my course requirement and my qualify exam for my dual Ph.D. program. The evaluation of the committee was that, even though I was not in my specialization and comfort area, I did do well on my qualify exam and was able to pass my exam. "I know he is not in his most comfortable area of the graduate coursework and research, but he was able to do well up to now," said Dr. Johnson. This made me so glad that I was able to handle and mange myself on the course work and research in the new area. Even through I was not in the comfort area, but I learned so much new information and was able to complete my dissertation work.

17

Our Picture of Life

Each of us all have available colors to paint our picture of life, so we need to paint in such a way that not only creates a great picture with balance of all the colors but a picture that expresses it own meaning (of life) so others can enjoy and be benefit from it.

Every one of us has our own picture of life. Our creator gives us all colors and tools to paint the picture of our own life. The color that we use and the design that we pick affects our own picture of life. Each moment we live will create dots and pieces of colors that paint and contribute to our final picture of life. So we need to paint our picture of life in a way that is not only good for our own life but also for others and serve our purpose and also our own desire while also having meaning. So our picture of life will express our personality and contribute to our society and make a positive effect and meaning in our own life and life of others.

Each hour, each minute, and each second are the gifts of life. So we need to spend widely and use it to paint our picture of life and use it to make the positive impact on others and our society.

Our feeling, our heart, will tell about ourselves, which controls the action of our daily activity. This then controls our picture and the pattern of our picture of life. So, we need to listen to our heart and our feelings to help us paint a quality picture of our life. The picture that tells the true meaning of life, the life of living a purpose and fulfillment of excitement and joyful.

We also need to keep in mind that our emotions control our action. So, when bad things happen, we need to control our emotions so we can handle these problems efficiently.

We live our life in pictures. So every moment, we capture displays some small segment of the current moment. These memories each hold an event or action of our thoughts, dreams, hopes, and beliefs in ourselves to paint a quality and effective picture of our life.

We live our life through a series of photographs in our daily life. These photographs form a parade of emotions. Highs and lows, good times and sad, in their totality they are what we have become. From an image of our family members that were celebrated and were around each others, helping us and each other through tough times and a great times.

18

Speak Great and Lovely Words Whenever You Can and Don't Wait Until We Do Not Have a Chance to Say These Words

Life is so short so speak the great and lovely words whenever you have a chance to say them and don't wait until you want to say them, but you don't have a chance to say it.

A lot of time, we do not realize what we have and until we lose it. Throughout my life, I experienced things and did not realize it until I lost it or once the situation is changing. Such as when we lost our family members or family falls apart. We need to pay attention to the things that happen around us. Things that are important. Like family members we normally do not realize the importance of each individual until we lose them, until the family member is no longer there. This is something we need to view in different angle. We always think things around us will always be there but we do not know what will happen. Things could happen in such a way that we never experience. We cannot know how the future turns out and we cannot fix the past, but we can live for the moment. We need to pay attention to those around us and enjoy it. Be a part of it and evolve with it. Every aspect of living, such as education, work, and relationships, one needs to participate and pay great attention to. If we don't constantly view and be part and try our best and live for the moment, we will regret it. If we already live and try our best and cannot do anything about it then we will let it going and will not look back at this bad thing as something that holds us back. In life sometimes, we can not tell who is right or who is wrong but our experiences and the way we interact and our behavior lead to the consequence of our own action.

The consequence and the way of how we act, how we interact, how we treat people around us, affect our inner peace and lead to the results of it. So the actions we take, our behavior, lead to the results of how we act. The ways we act, the way we interact, will lead to the end results and impact the people around us. The emotions, the feelings and acting in such a good way will create a ripple, stimulate and create a feeling and ripple with and around others. Like a drop of water in a lake creates such a ripple and creates a beautiful image of a wave on the water's surface. In life our feeling of one of us, such like an initiation of the group of communities, there is a great idea of such individuals to serve and do great for communities and they will create an impact on others and they will get attention with others who also join the group to create and provide great things or volunteer and provide service and good for other people, such as the poor, with others. I remember, one time we started to donate and give money to the poor. We not only can help people but other people also participate and we end up with greater contribution to the poor and provide more help to the poor.

Buda said, *"The root of every cause if it comes from ourselves, how we act, it effects thing that happened around us."* So our action and thing whether bad or great action all come from us and we have the full control of it.

Similarly, I was taught a little from God's message that we are to, "Love our neighbor as ourselves." We do love people, be nice for people around us, try to heal and give those who are poor food and to whoever and however we can. Sometimes it is not by money or food but only a word can help and make other people feel great, feel happy, and not lonely in life. Because we also know that we need to help people who are not so lucky or those who are not able to help and serve. *By the end of the day, we find ourselves and ask what have we been doing for us and for people around us.*

Each day, I try to pray to God and spend some silent time to thinking about what I have been doing for that day. I remind myself what I have done for that day so I can improve myself. For those days that I did something good, I need to say, "Thanks God for what you helped me do, this great thing."

Each morning when I wake up, I try to thank God for another good day that I live on this planet. So I need to do great things for it, for my benefit, and the benefit of people around me.

When I say thanks for each minute that I live on this planet, I start to review myself in such as way I never experienced. I start to pray before I eat. Thank God for the food we eat. I start to feel blessed and happier and possible things around us. "Thank you, God and thank you for my entire family, every member, for always being there for me."

I started to change and also look at how my life was up to now. I started to review the importance of life. The most important thing is being around people you love and your family members. I thank our parents who gave birth to me, raised me, and have always been there for me. Thanks to my brothers and sister for always being there for me. Being there at my lowest and in my most happy and in my saddest time in my life. And thanks, Mom and Dad, and everyone who is in my life. Thanks to those who left a great footprint in my life and who challenged me so I can grow and who have been there for me and supported me so I can be who I am today. Thank you for those who are there, who have been through life with me, who will always be there for me. And always share my happiness and my sorrowful times with me.

Our Culture

Traditional Vietnamese culture doesn't say or express emotions or say thank you as much and this is often happening in our family and around our environment. When we grow older, we normally tend not to say thanks when we receive something or when our family members or our Mom does something for us. Our traditions, and my Dad, really hardly say thanks to us. This is common and typical in our tradition. Because deep in my heart I know that we appreciate it, but sometimes we just do not say it in words. This makes me usually tend to become more silent. We need to say thanks and say to these who help us, to who have done great thing to us and even small things. We also constantly need to thank God as well, thank each and everyone, every action, and everything that they have done for us.

The more I interact with people, and the more I learn, I feel that, we need to say thank you, so it helps us interact and bond with our family members, with people whom we love. Unlike the traditional Vietnam culture, the Western or American culture is more expressive by saying thank you to every member when each member has done something for them and also in return in the family and outside the family. This is the different between traditional American culture and for typical Vietnamese culture.

When I lose my family members, such as my grandmother and grandfather, I realize this loss changed things and my behavior; I started to appreciate each and every action and things they have done for me. I started to thank my Mom more whenever she prepares a meal for me or helps me and for always being there for me.

I felt and realized that I really owe thanks to my Mom for being there for me, for us, and for our family.

Each week that I was away for school and work, I came home to my parents and my Mom always prepared something for me. "Let me make you some spring rolls," said Mom. When I traveled away from home, I really missed these words. I started to realize the importance of my Mom in my life. I started to appreciate more, appreciate and have the feeling of being at home, being able to appreciate these things more that I am suppose to say and thank her for them. I feel more complete and more appreciative of these things and these meals that my Mom prepared for me. I stared to say thank you to my Mom more often.

"Thank you, Mom for the meal," I said. I thank you, Mom, for the meal. I feel that being a person away from home, being away from the normal things helps us to view them in a different prospective, different angle, and we tend to realize and experience things in such way that we have been through and think. This also helps me and strengthens me. We know that we build our confident from dedication and hard work. So, through dedication, we can improve ourselves, improve our mentality, and our personality.

19

Our Mind and It's Behaviors

All of our actions and behavior is the consequence of our responding from our mind. The behavior of our mind is the consequent of things we interact with and things we observe, feels from both our inner self and the environment around us. So, we learn to control ourselves by learning to control our deep inner self so we can control our repose and behavior.

Everyone seems to have a clear idea of how other people should lead their lives, but none of his or her own. The only way to understand ourselves is listened to our conscience. Constantly listening to our heart each second, each minute, and each day to find out what we want. We need to know what we want and also see things from our own perspective and then view things from different perspectives if we can.

Quiet places help us to think, to realize more things about and around us. Realizing more what we have been doing, what we have been through, and improve our mentality and personality. Improving our inner peace and our strength.

But through suffering and tragedy, we define our personality. This is because through this tragedy and suffering, it defines the way we act. The way we act is impacted in our thoughts and we constantly react to our actions.

Through bad situations or activity, our mind will define and find the way we act, the way we act and actions will define the results. So, all the results and the way we act are the consequences and are the results of our mind, and our behavior. So our mind controls all the actions that we take and the entire thing that we want to achieve. So in life, we need to give ourselves a goal and purpose and recreate our mind with new desires and ideas so it can respond and do things that right and fit for us, for our purpose in life.

If we think good thoughts and act well, our surroundings and the world will respond with great things for us. So our mind controls our actions and the actions effected the nature and impact things around us. The nature then responds to the way we act. If we act in such a great way, the nature will respond to us with great and positive actions. This is the law of attraction that we all know from school, that what we act we will get, or what we want to ask nature, nature will respond to what we want. It is similar to a wave, an amplitude of the wave. Only the right frequency will receive it and will respond to it.

20

Each of Us Has Our Own Greatness

The Epiphyllum flower only blooms one time for one hour and only in the nighttime, but it gives a bloom so well, so beautiful, and so spectacular. Such are each of us when go through tough times to reach our final destination, our final goal, but each of us have our own greatness, our own specialty.

Epiphyllum flower in VietNam and Minosa Pudica follower

Epiphyllum flower (or Hoa Quỳnh as they called in Vietnam) represents the "beauty faithful" (loyal beauty), for flowers bloom only once and then are ruined, as well as a first love original and unique offering for the centennial.

Enjoying the blooming of the Epiphyllum flower is so special and joyful. In the ancient traditions, whenever they know the flower is about to bloom, they invite a few friends to enjoy. Pending the enjoyment of watching the flowers bloom, we made a pot of tea truth. The delicious, fragrant smoke spiraling up, while we are just sipping, waiting on the blossoms and admiring the beauty of a flower so special. The Epiphyllum flower only blooms one time for one hour and only in the nighttime, but it gives the bloom so well, so beautiful and so spectacular.

Unlike Epiphyllum flower, Minosa Pudica is well known for its rapid plant movement. Like a number of other plant species, it undergoes changes in leaf orientation termed "sleep" or nyctinastic movement. The foliage closes during darkness and reopens in light. The leaves also close under various other stimuli, such as touching, warming, blowing, or shaking. For this special feature, in VietNam it also has the name as Hoa Trinh Nữ or "Virgin Flower." It is just like a shy virgin girl. These two flowers have their own greatness and their own special attributes.

As discussed, these two special flowers have their own features, each of us also has our own special greatness. Each of us has our own greatness and our own strength. None of us are like each other. We need to know what our strengths and our weaknesses are. As a human, we have capabilities and can accomplish the thing that we want to. Each of us has our own strengths. These strengths could be improved upon by practice. We need to express these strengths so we can improve and stand out. We have the ability to adapt to a new environment and also can change our own environment. So we need to find a way to improve the environment or done to the environment so it can improve our living standards and quality of our living, and living with purpose.

As a human being, we have the ability to observe, to recognize, and think about things around us. This ability makes us able to see greatness and strength in other people. We can see and recognize strength, greatness, and talents from others. We encourage them to take action, to listen to their hearts, follow their dreams, and try to accomplish the things that they want to do. We can easily recognize these and see these talents from people, but it is harder to recognize our own. This is because we tend to be affected by things around us. Things that are happening around us. We are an effect of the sound, the voice from others, but not much of our own.

Our culture trains us to not tell or express much or tell others that,"I am good at this and I am good at that." It is the way of our culture; we hide our own greatness and our own talent. That's why only others are easy to see and observe our own greatness and our own talent.

We recognize our greatness, which means believing that, "We are all great." Which mean both you and I. We all have our own greatness. Once we recognize it, we can improve our greatness, our special talent or skills.

We could express and find out what is our greatness and talent by asking ourselves and making a list. What are your talents? What makes you special? What are you really good at? What are others saying is good about you? What other things about you do people enjoy? Be honest to yourself so you know what is truly your specialness and your greatness.

As a little child, I did not have a chance to practice and play an instrument, but recently, I had the chance to be exposed to an instrument. I was able to learn and play several instruments by myself in a short period of time. This is to show that, we may not able to express our skill and talent if we do not give ourselves a chance to express it. It is just the same with any other skill, talent, strength, and greatness. If we do not give ourselves and think we have it; we will not be able to express it and see it from our own perspective.

21

The Predestinated Affinity Has Begun, Then Another Once Should End

"You must remain open for mercy. Forgive beings, no matter how bad they are, even if they hurt you, you have to let go, to get real joy"
Buddha's teachings in life

If such thing in life begins certainly, then they should be ended with certainty. A new life started, another life should be ended. So life is just a cycle if one life began, another life should be ended. This not only talking about things that are happening in our life, but also talking about our life in general.

We need to let things go naturally, and go on in the way it is by itself, and do not do the things and are different directions that effect or damage ourselves. By definition that is the way it should be in life; then we can chose and pick up our path and follow our path without regretting that we picked the wrong path.

Everything in life is such that we meet someone, things happen in our life with predestinated affinity. So, we come into this world, we will have our own destination.

When we think about our final destination, we only normally think much about what we have accomplished, and do not talk about our life, or the end our life, end of out path, or end life. According to Buddhism, our lives and all that occur in our lives is a result of karma. Every action creates a new karma; this karma or action is created with our body, our speech, or our mind, and this action leaves a subtle imprint on our mind, which has the potential to ripen as future happiness or future suffering, depending on whether the action was positive or negative. If we bring happiness to people, we will be happy. If we create suffering, we will experience suffering either in this life or in a future one.

The situation in life and karma is analogous to a famous story of the businessman who starts his business at the beginning of the year. At the end of the year, he has to account for his profit and loss, repay all his debts, and get back what others owe him. The process repeats the following year and every year after that. In the end, the businessman plans to accumulate long term profits.

The final profit depends on the following year's, depends on the current year's business profitable. Everything will run more smoothly next year if this year has more profit. And if this year results in a loss, then next year's financial position will be tight. And we may need to borrow from here or there and create more worry and frustration and suffering for ourselves.

Our life and karma are the same. When there is birth, there will be death. During the process of life and death, we have to consider our profits and losses. We improve ourselves and become a better person in this life, then we will create good prospects for our future.

By definition, if there is karma or something happening or beginning, then there should be something ending. As a great human body, we have to accept our path, accept things that happen in life, live with it, and enjoy the beauty that this life gives and create for us and enjoy our path. If we think and have general ideas in life and accept it with peace, then we can chose and pick up our path and follow our path without regret for picking the wrong path. But the most important thing is making sure we can make a profit by improving our life, not only creating good and prosperity but also doing good to others and society.

22

Is It Right That You Do Not Realize What You Have Until You Lose It?

We tend to not know what we have until we have lost it. After these lose, we tend to realize it and need to work hard to pick up those that we lose. As long as we do not lose our path, our desire everything else is not very important.

Lonely bird at Alki Beach in Seattle

Is it right that you do not realize what you had until you have lost it? Throughout these years of my busy time, I did not realize it until now. It's a feeling I have felt recently. Life has changed, and everything around me seems to have changed. Since then, I appreciate things around me more and value them more. Due to these losses and the whole experience, they have made me more mature, respectful, and appreciative of the things I have around me. I crave a family gathering for a meal with my family. My cravings are to share a cake with someone or likewise to have somebody to do normal work with together such as laundry each week. I have cravings for being together to prepare a simple meal and to eat together. For me, now this is very difficult and hard to obtain. I have cravings for someone to walk along the beach with and to see the sunset in the afternoon each day to see and share moments together in life and to experience life together.

We Go Through Suffering and Tragedy. Then We Will Realize What Went Wrong

We do not know what we have until we lose it. We also realize what went wrong or normally do not realize this until after we went through suffering.

As a human, we normally did not experience or fully know exactly what we have, what is important in our life, and what is most important for us. The most valuable and important things can be changed from each stage of our lives. But we usually don't realize this until we lose it or until we are in a different situation or have a different prospective. Just like a great example of a person who is on the boat with waves and wind and he still cries and yells but when he falls once into the ocean with no one to help him, so he knows that he only needs someone to help him, to serve him, because he may die by drowning. Once he got someone to pick him up to the boat, he felt that being in the boat is a better stage and never cries or yells again. So, our human mind will hardly experience or know if we are in a tougher stage when we experience it. Once we experience it and see the difference then we tend to learn and realize that we are already in the great stage. So we are always in the great stage but a lot of times we do not know it. Therefore, we need to enjoy the stage that we are in at the moment. So we can value that we are still living in this life and enjoy the beauty of the world given to us.

23

Review Our Own Root

We can review ourselves and go back to our own place to compare and view these changes. Seeking the image of ourselves and how things change. We will experience what we have done and gain so much and a deeper perspective about ourselves and how you see the things around us.

In front of Ben Thanh market (one of the oldest market in Sai Gon) and Our Lady of Lord Church

Everyone who has never lived in Saigon and went to a different city or is living in a different country, will think of Saigon as having hot weather and so much noise. It is true when I was back in Saigon. However, but I can manage the weather. Once we can manage the weather, then we can enjoy the beauty and fun of it.

"We are about 30 minutes from landing, please keep your seatbelt buckled and do not walk the aisle or use the toilet. We are decreasing altitude and preparing to land. The weather in Saigon now is approximately 80 degrees. Thank you very much for flying with us. We would love to serve you in the near future," said the pilot.

Everybody in the airplane is really looking forward to the landing. I am also really look forward to it. And finally we are landing. I really missed Saigon. After over 22 years. I came back with so much emotion, emotions of coming back to my own country, my own roof, visiting the place where I grew up. Visiting my own country with my people and culture. I have so much feelings and really emotions about visiting my country with a lot of feelings that I have been back since I left. When I left the country, I though that it would be very hard to go back and visit the country. But now I have a chance to go back, to see the changes, and to remind myself of the country and the place that I was born and grew up with. There is so much joy and happiness to be back.

Who has ever left the country for over 20 years and then come back to visit? There are so many changes and review the place where I was born. All the memories from when I was a kid suddenly comes back. Each of us has memories with our own place in our own town and the place we grew up and with so much joy and memories. It is the place where we belonged. Each of us all have been able to adapt and fit into the new place, new country, but we also remember our own country and our own ancestors. Because this is the cause of our freedom and opportunities, we have to remember.

We came back with the feeling that we have grown up and now really see the changes and to review our roof, our ancestors. We all have great feelings of coming back and seeing the changes in our town and the changes and to reflect on ourselves. I start to review myself, see the changes, hear the noise, visit places that I have never been. I started to feel Vietnam also has many beautiful places that I did not have a chance to explore when I was young.

Beautiful beach in Vinpearl Island and HaLong Bay in VietNam

24

The Harvest Time is the Happiest For the Farmer

The peaceful life of the farmers and their harvest time create a joy and happiness that they value their work. Each of us will have our on destination and our own way of service in this life. But life should be full of happiness and enjoyment. Farmer life is a simple life that creates a peaceful time throughout for each member of the family.

Each end of the year during the middle of December is the rice harvest season. There are so many happy times with people gathering to harvest the rice. In the rice field, it's full of wheat that has turned yellow. The harvest time is normally so happy because we had been working hard, and it is time to pick up the results of it. But the amount of wheat to obtain also depends on the weather during the growing time. The quality of wheat also depends on the weather, soil, and water level.

So the life of the farmer depends on the weather during the year that produces the amount of rice. However, their life is so peaceful, simple, and easy. The morning starts earlier than most of the people in the city. The working day starts much earlier, before the sunrise. They gather and drink coffee or tea with such happy faces to start the workday.

"Good morning," said the worker to the owner. The workers are gathering and starting to work for the owner. However, there is no pushing of the owner; he lets them start to work and have their breaks on their own when needed. The working environment is full with fun and enjoyment. Everyone talks to each other and has so much fun. Each can work on or do what their ability allows in their own specialty area. Wheat was cut then collected and tied with hay and carried on with the kayak. Depending on the area, The area in the Delta Mekong normally can carries with kayaks to other areas of the rice field and the areas without river then it can be carried by machine or small hand push carrier.

Once we are at the harvest with harvest activities, we will feel amazing at the level of joy and happiness that the farmers expressed.

Rice field in one of the branch of Delta Me Kong
River and activities during the harvest day

At each end of the work day during the harvest time, each individual on the work team all gather and drink and express the emotions, the feeling of joy and even sing. *The life is simple and so peaceful. I have observed the excitement and joyfulness of them and concluded that no mater what life or what path we take, when you're with family and loved ones and can do things you like, enjoy the moments you have; then we feel that we live for a purpose no matter if our life is full of material things or filled with a lot of money and abundant or no materials.*

25

God's Message

"Love your neighbor as yourself," Jesus' words

If we are living with God's message, love our neighbor as ourselves, we will create an environment full of love. With no hating or doing things that are harmful to others or to nature. By living God's way, there will be no violence in this world.

No matter where you come from, who you are, we all have our personal path. By experiencing daily activities and this great words from God or from Buda, this makes us think more about ourselves, our purpose, our mission in life. The message from God helps us to slow down, think about what our living purpose is, our destination. We all have a goal and are living for a purpose, but we need to review ourselves by seeking through others. One great way of seeking ourselves, is the view of things around us, our neighbor, or our family. This way helps each and every one of us think and live with a purpose.

The powerful creator can lead us, to make us calm and focused on ourselves. Focusing more about ourselves and our inner peace than the external forces and things that impact us daily. The inner peace has much importance and impact on us. So daily activities, such as reading the Bible or reaching God's world or Buda's world helps me to calm down and stay focus on my goal and purpose.

One of my difficult times when I was an undergraduate student at UW was to wake up very early each day and stay late at school until almost midnight, but also to stay focused on school, coursework, and also work after school each day. By reading the Bible, praying, and meditating each day, this helped me release a lot of stress and keep me peace and focus. Each end of the school day, or even during study time at the library, I tried to meditate and read the Bible at lease 15 minutes.

One of the greatest stories that I really admire is about the Cardinal Xiave Nguyen Van Thuan. He had been spending time in the communist camp and isolated himself for eight years. With living the purpose of service to God, he can serve and even help the officer to live with a purpose, help him to reflect upon himself, and live with peace and with the message from God by loving your neighbor as yourself.

Another story from Saint Paul IIX is that he went to and visited the person who tried to kill him. He forgave that person. He tried to release that person from prison. That person really admire him and admitted his sin and changed his view and became a better person.

***

Is there a way to break free from what is still holding you back? Is there a key to unlock this way for you? And how do you start? What is the first step? What comes next?

I believe that there is a personal path, regardless of were you come from or where you are. And it's not just fate or luck. I believe and know from my own experience that it's very straightforward: a step-by-step process that is still very individual but everybody can go through to realize his potential in each stage in life. But what we need is a guide through those steps, something that helps us authentically to build that way.

26

Stages of Life That Each of Us Needs to Go Through

Each of us will go through all stages in our life, but sometimes we forget and never look back because in time we all always forgot that, each of us has around 65 years to live, or even less, but time is flying by so fast and sometimes we do not even realize it. And each at each stage of our lives, our thinking and mindset will be different. Our view of others and things around us are also different.

From what I have experienced and learned, we have about six stages that make us most scared and we need to go through in life, that most of us remember and are so scary for. They are: infancy, puberty, accomplishment, midlife, late adulthood, and death/dying.

1. Stage of Infancy (ages of 0-3): In this stage, the thing that we are scared of is we start learning how to walk and experience things around us as we first learn how to walk during this stage and fall. Depending on the person, we may have recall of things that we have been through that scared us and some memories.

2. Stage of puberty (age of 13-18): As we went through puberty, things changed with our body and our feelings changed. This made us scared and afraid of things changing in ourselves.

3. Accomplishment stage (18-35): It could vary from person to person because, for some people with experience and leaving school early, they could experience this stage earlier. Depending on people who have a good foundation and preparation for such events as getting an education, finding that they can fit into

this world and society and be valued, contribute and be part of society. If they have a great education or great career, then they are more easily able to fit into society and they are less scared or worried, compared to those who go through life uneducated and do not have special skills to contribute or be part of the society.

4. Midlife (ages 35-50): After many years in young adulthood and following society's scripting for creating a life, a family, a career. People in midlife often take a break or take a different view and perspective and try to do different things to enrich their life and sometimes look at ways to change their daily and normal activities. This also effect family and most couples do things and change their view and effect the family and families fall apart and divorce happens in this stage.

5. Late Adulthood (age 50 and older): At this stage, we have acquired a rich repository of experiences that we can use to help guide others. People in this stage tend to give advice and guide other, and like to talk to others especially to those younger who listen to them.

6. Death & Dying: This is the stage in our living that we are so scare of because in this state of our lives we are dying. People in this stage teach us about the values of living. For these are people who have a peaceful life; they can pass this life with peace. Because we constantly do not know what is happening and where we are going.

So depending on the different stages we went through, our thinking, worries, fears, and the values or importance of things we value are different. And what we experience and leave behind and how we respond to others are also different. However, as we get older, we tend to remember only the major event that happened in our life not how old we are. And this is the reason why some young people might have great prospective in life because they already went through some of these even in life. They are able to understand about different stages in life and their concern or thoughts in different stages help them easily understand and to communicate with others. Thus, helping them gain more happiness.

My Grandmother Passing Away

I was there for my grandmother passing away. Max, my younger brother, and I were reading the Bible to help my grandmother during her dying period. There are prayers that we normally read for people when they are dying to review and make their passing and dying in peace or at least help them stay calm and die peacefully.

"Our Father who art in heaven,: hallowed be thy name. Thy kingdom come. Thy will be done: on earth as it is in heaven. Give us this day our daily bread..." and so on, Max and I keep reading.

"Grandmother past away" or "Bà ngoại đi rồi in VietNamese", my Dad cried out loud to bring my Mom and my uncle and all of us in the house to attention.

My Dad, said he felt (and saw) the spirit that left when my grandmother was passing. We were experiencing so much loss and sadness in all of our family members for the loss of my grandmother.

Several days later, I was busy involved with my aunt in the preparations and plans for my grandmother's funeral ceremony at the funeral house and at the church, and finally at the Holyrood Cemetery.

***

I still remember each time my grandmother talked about the tragedy when I was little when my Mom was paralyzed and cried every time. Each year, I still visit her grave in Lynwood, WA.

27

Each Day, Each Minute, Each Breath is the Gift of Life

Each day, each minute, each breath is the gift of life, so we need to spend it greatly.

Beautiful Vinpear beach in VietNam and Space Needle in Seatlle, WA USA

What will we feel if we are living our life with our heart waiting to stop at any minute? That is the case of one of my friend's sister.

"Quan already passed away," Huan said with a very emotional voice to me.

"Wow really? How come and why?" with a sad voice, I asked Huan. I really feel sad about this. Quan was a very great friend that I met when I went to the US and we went to Chief Sealth High School with. After I went to UW and did not have much time and to hang out and keep in touch with Quan. Huan said Quan met several new friends and was hanging out with them where he normally went to drink and his heart was not able to handle that level of stimulate or stress and his heart stopped. The second time his hear stopped, doctors were not able to get it back up again. Quan knew of his heart problems but he still enjoying and have a normal life. He passed when he was less than 30 years old.

The story does not stop until I heard that his sister was also waiting for her heart transplant. She had been waiting for so long for the new heart to replace hers. His sister, Nga, was a great computer engineering major that went to UW and we were normally carpooling together during the second and third years of my undergraduate studies. But the difference is that, her sister had so much motivation, but even she could not do many things like normal people do, such as give birth or go to anything stressful and do such activities or sport as other people. I recently checked with her sister and she finally got her heart transplant and is waiting for recovery.

***

Whenever we have joy or we can open our heart and accept and enjoy things around us, we are then able to live a life with full and abundant joy and happiness. We are living in this planet and have so much happiness and joy.

When we know that each day, each minute, and each breath is a gift of life, then we will not waste any minutes. We then use it wisely. We then think of the most important things that we need to accomplish in this life and things that we want to do so they have more meaning in life and benefit to others and make such positive impact on others around us.

I have been travelling to different places, different countries, to see different things, different places, and enjoy the beauty of nature. Only when I experience and have been through this will you experience the joy and the emotion. I remember that a lot of people talk about New York, Times Square, Manhattan in New York and Last Vegas and so on and on. I was not able to experience these places until I stood there and saw the place myself, I did not see and experience the emotions. When I was on the tour at Liberty Helicopter to view all around Manhattan and New York City, seeing the Statue of Liberty, I was able to experience the emotion and really view how beautiful these places are, and see that there are so may things in life that we can enjoy and we should spend our life wisely. When standing on the streets and seeing Manhattan and Times Square on the street, we only view one angle or one view of it. When viewing Manhattan from a helicopter, we see the city so beautiful and full of energy with cars and people walking around and moving on the streets. I can see the Statue of Liberty on the small island, this created a spectacular and beautiful picture and image of New York City. The city view was so also pretty from the Empire State Building. There are so many tall buildings that we can only imagine. When looking at it, I appreciate the nature and admire how creative the human mind is because with our mind and out commitment, we can build such an incredible bridge as the Brooklyn Bridge and such buildings as the Empire State Building. I very much admire the creativity of our human mind and the ability to work together and organize such an amazing project to build such an amazing building and bridge.

28

We Need to Start to Go Today In Order to Reach the Destination Tomorrow

If we want to reach the destination tomorrow, we need to start as early as today. To reach any goals or anything in life, we need to plan, have a goal, have a way, and to develop the way to obtain it.

We study, we need to find out what we want to become, we need to have a place to study (the environment), the place to study and the ability (our strength) to get it. We need to fully look at ourselves, what we are good at. Things that we are able to do, things that we are weak on. And things that we need to work on to improve.

In life, every one of us needs to start even through we do not want to start out, our life still start by itself. In order to reach out or reach some where tomorrow or in the future, we need to start out and make an action today. There will be nothing to be done if we just talk about it and never get it to the action and start to work on it. Such is the same for school. If we do not start school in the first grade and finish high school and college and go further to graduate school and so on, then we are never able to reach into college and university.

In life, along with the things we start out liking, we also find new and interesting things along the way or along our path. To accomplish and reach into different stages and levels in life, we need to start at the bottom first and work our way up. There are no shortcuts in the middle. There are lots of things in life that we can finish earlier, but we cannot take a shortcut in life.

As we develop our path and our own motivation, we come to an understanding that our path to final goals, to our final destination in life is to fulfill our goal and our dream of doing and finishing things in life. In life there are so many things that we want to accomplish and to finish, therefore we always need to start as early as possible and finish and reach our end goal as soon as possible.

We must start to take action and to follow our hearts and follow our path and to finish and reach our final destination.

Just as any sport and playing an instrument, we need to start to learn and keep practicing to play it. We then become more familiar with things and then eventually we can become experts with these particular sports and instruments. If we just wait and do not start to involve ourselves and to pick up these as early as possible then time will fly by and we will regret not trying it or not starting it in the first place.

Have you ever wondered and asked yourself, if I had started that thing or if I did that then now I would be different and better to prepared myself like someone you see who has done something in life. As we go back and review our childhood dream, we normally change and do not keep our dreams all the time. Is this because we cannot do it or simply because we just do not start it? Even if we started on it and later we find out that we cannot do it or we just cannot fit into it, we will not regret it ourselves in the future. Just like when I wanted to go start medical school but I found out later on that it was not a good fit for me. Even though I did not complete it, I still feel that I already started and tried it and do not regret that I did not try in the first place.

29

The Journey of Success

No matter who we are and whether we pick our own path or not, we still need to follow one path in life. The path may lead us to darkness or up and down with happiness and sorrow but as we manage and keep continuing our path or even take different paths with much longer or shorter distances, we still can reach our final destination.

In 2001, I was normally travelling back and forth to Pacific Northwest National Laboratory (PNNL) in Richland, Washington to work for my fellowship. It took about five hours of driving and normally I traveled from Seattle to PNNL at evening time on Sunday. During the weekend in Seattle, I had to work on the house remodeling. I usually got very tired when I got to my place there. There were a couple of paths that I could take around Yakima and I had to pass through several mountains. I normally traveled without a break in the middle. I really got tired when I was passing Yakima and usually felt very sleepy. The road normally got very dark and there were no streetlights. I started to follow any cars that I saw that could lead me or at least to see the road because my headlights were not so bright and especially since I had to wear glasses and it was during the night that I was traveling. I would follow almost any cars along the way to help me see the road well, but sometimes the cars I followed traveled too fast or too slow, then I could not use them to guide or lead me. I needed to find a car with a similar driving speed to follow. But I cannot follow it too far when these cars went in a different direction or exit the freeway and I needed to make a turn or keep on the same path because there were two paths that lead me to Richland and I needed to pass Yakima and passing these high mountain on a very dark road which was very hard to drive. Most of the time, if I made a turn to pick one path to Richland, then I could not follow the car in front of me or at least that car can lead me out of some of the dark road because the car in front of me did not pick the road that I did. And because sometimes the car I followed did not take the turn, but it exited to Yakima then it could not even help me or guide me through these mountains. But some how along these paths on either one I took, I always managed to reach Richland. Whenever I saw houses with lights and saw the city, I felt very relieved because I felt that I survived travelling that night. There are several times I felt it was not safe for traveling. One time I almost drove over the side or hit these pole along the side on the freeway but it is like a journey that I needed to take, a path through these dark, high mountains and see these lights of the city before I reached my place.

***

The place that I roomed at, I was introduced to from a person that I found from a local ad. During my first time to travel the lady told me that I needed to meet the owner at their place at 7:30pm to start the lease. On my first Sunday, I packed everything that I needed and traveled there, but when I traveled there, I was late for the meeting time and back in 2001, I did not even have cell phone to let the owner know. I was half-an-hour late, and when I got there nobody was there. With all the effort for travelling almost five hours to pass all the dark roads and pass these mountains, I reached the final destination, but I could not meet the owner and it was so dark and there was not much house around that has the light on. I was waiting for a while and started to cry with so much worry and waited and waited for another hour and finally the owner showed up and I was able to enter the house.

The traveling was longer than I thought, and I felt so tired and started to realize that all the worry cannot wither my desire and my motivation. I also learned to let our hearts open and accept thing that are happening along the way and along our road. No matter which road you take, you will end and reach your final destination. I also learned that life is an adventure; there are ups and down but with the desire and motivation and never giving up, we will reach our final destination.

***

In 2007, after I finished my Masters, I would like to go to get an MD degree and thought that I would go for PhD after I finished my MD. Because, I got a double bachelors degree, one in Chemistry and one in Engineering, I was able to fulfill my requirement of organic chemistry for the chemistry requirement. However, I need three courses of general biology. At UW, at the graduate school all the 200 level classes and below, there are no grades; my entire grade in biology is just blank and I was not able to apply to any locally medical school. The only school that would accept this was St. Mathew Medical School at Grand Cayman Island. I started my MD schooling and thought that I would be able to finish it and be able to go and get my Ph.D. as well. But I did not have any background in anatomy and not much in biological science. I was trained in engineering without much memory like medical school and especially in anatomy. I was having trouble in these courses and there was so much memorization and the environment was very hard and different than when I was in graduate school. I did not have much respect. At graduate school, I was teaching chemistry and materials engineering courses, but once I was at St. Mathew Medical School, I was not really got respected and treated as a freshman in college.

After almost a year, I went back to exactly the same place where I left off and worked on my dual PhDs. But I learned so many things and experienced so much that I never experienced before in terms of life, family, and friendship. I met so many wonderful lifetime friends there.

30

Next

"Develop success from failures. Discouragement and failure are two of the surest stepping stones to success." By Dale Carnegie, author of one of the most famous book, How to Win Friends and Influence People.

When thinking about my life when I was young and up to now, I almost died and almost did not get together with my parents and grow up. I was able to pass all the hard courses in Vietnam where I was a countryside student and only I was able to pass my high school. My life turned to a different path when I left Vietnam at the age of 18 and went to several schools and finished, though one I did not finish, and I received a couple of bachelor degrees, master, and double PhDs. I also have many turns and paths in my life, such as my family falling apart, I lost lots of money in real estate during the economic recession in 2006. I lost my first job just after completing my PhD, but I was able to go through these things and experiences so many things that I never experienced before. I now feel that my life is in the next stage with so much energy and experiences that help me through tough times and bad times.

We need to live our life in a way that we do not have to feel regret or sorry for it. Each of us needs to do something that we value and things that are a benefit to our society, but we need to remind ourselves that, we do not have all the time we want. None of us knows how long we will live. So time is limited. There are limits in our life and our time in this world. So our picture of life needs to be painted in such a way that we can feel great once we leave this life.

We also need to start our path and start out our life even though we do not want to choose or even we do not want to start it. Once we are in this life, we already automatically have a path, have a life to start, have a goal, and have to reach our final destination. Each of us has our own path, our own destination, but we still need to reach our final end mark, our final goal. So, we grow older and older, we need to listen and think more about ourselves, our inner peace, and our mind, and our heart, see what we want to, how we want to get to the next level. How do we need to get to the level we want to be?

In life, our final destination is not determined by how much money we make, how many material possessions we accumulate, or how successful we are at work. It is determined by how much peace we have in our life and in our mind.

Acknowledgements

I would like to humbly acknowledge the love and support that I have received from a number of wonderful people; without them, I could not have completed this manuscript and make this through in my life. It is with great pleasure that I would like to take this opportunity to express my sincere appreciation to all those who have helped me throughout this process, through out bad times and also being around in my life and helping me throughout these difficult times.

First and foremost, I owe my deepest gratitude to my Mom and Dad, for the love and unconditional support to pursue my interests. They worked so hard to raise me and my siblings during and after the Vietnam War. I sincerely acknowledge my mother for her hard work, including the sacrifices for us while my Dad was in the communist education camp for many years. I would like to thank my Dad, who spent many years in the terrible camp, for his services during the war, and for enduring the many tragedies that he went through. I would like to thank my grandmother who already past away for the inspiration, my aunt, Dao Bui for her endless encouragement, my uncle, Professor Den Truong at North Carolina State University for his support and constant guidance, my brothers and sister, Hoai Le, Thuy-Huong Le, Ho-Hoai Le, Dr. Joshua Le, and Max Le for their continuous support and always putting up with me even when I was unreasonable.

Second, I would like to thank Kayly for her love, support, enduring, challenging, understanding and taking care of our lovely daughter so I can spend more time on this manuscript. We have so many great times together. I also learned the most valuable lesson in life and in relationships.

I would like to thank Mong Tuyen for her inspiration, to help me understand and to review my love, her motivation and encouraging me so I can finish the manuscript. I also would like to thank Kim Le for helping with images and the book cover. Thank you very much to Phuong-Anh, Mr. Dung Thai Bui, and Mr. Ghi Dang for willing to share images.

Third, I would like to thank my lovely daughter for her inspiration and for her understanding so that I can be away from home to spend time to work on this manuscript. Thanks for having so much time since the day you were born until now. We have so many great times together; I still remember the day you were born to the day I taught you how to swim and to today. It is always great to be around you and you are the reason for I continue. One day when you are old enough, you will understand why I had to be away and did not spend much time with you as I would like. You will also understand that I have a difficult path and been through many tough and difficult situations. Daddy always loves you no matter what happen.

Last but not least, thanks Milo at OSU for valuable life lessons and being around me. Many thanks to all my fellow friends at OSU, UW, St. Mathew Medical School, for being around, encourage me or staying up with me throughout these years. Special thanks to many faculties and staffs at UW and OSU to help and encourage me throughout these years.

Finally, I would like to thank God, for always being there, for His love and for being there with me through the great times and through the bad times. Through Him, I am now able to find and understand my purpose and my mission in life.

Printed in the United States
By Bookmasters